TRUE CRIMES

UNDYING LOVE

igloo

igloo

This edition published in 2010
by Igloo Books Ltd
Cottage Farm
Sywell
NN6 0BJ

www.igloo-books.com

Copyright © 2009 Igloo Books Ltd

A copy of the British Library Cataloguing-in-Publication
Data is available from the British Library.

10 9 8 7 6 5 4 3 2 1

ISBN 978-0-85734-397-0

Printed and Manufactured in China

Contents

Millicent Adams

The case of Millicent Adams is a classic example of what can happen when a woman in love is treated with contempt by her lover. What is unusual about it is that even though Millicent freely admitted killing Axel Schmidt, her sentence was as light as the court could possibly impose while still seeming to punish her.

The daughter of a wealthy and respected Philadelphia family, the misfortunes of Millicent Adams began at Bryn Mawr University in the early 1960s where she met and fell in love with fellow student Axel Schmidt. Although he was studying to be an engineer, it occurred to Schmidt that a faster route to the wealth and the glittering social life he dreamed of might be through marriage, and he tirelessly courted Millicent until another girl came along whose family was even more wealthy and prominent than hers. With richer pickings on offer, Schmidt quickly dumped Millicent. As she later told police, she had been so hurt that she just wanted to kill herself.

BELOW: A Smith And Wesson Ladysmith .22 revolver, similar to the one used by Millicent Adams.

In preparation for her suicide Millicent bought a large St. Bernard dog, then took it to an unused room in her parents' mansion and shot it with a .22 caliber Smith & Wesson pistol. She explained during questioning that she wanted to be sure that it worked when she turned it upon herself. But it wasn't Millicent that ended up dead. With the promise of farewell sex in the air, she lured Schmidt to her home and after inviting him into her bed fired a single bullet and killed him. If she had been thinking about suicide before, she seemed to have forgotten about it now, for she didn't shoot herself after all. It may have been the knowledge that she was carrying Schmidt's child which stopped her pulling the trigger.

At her trial, Millicent's defense argued that she had acted in a moment of insanity caused by her lover's cold treatment of her. The court agreed that she should be allowed to plead guilty to manslaughter and not murder and, when she was pronounced guilty, gave her a ten-year probational sentence on condition that she admitted herself to a mental health institution.

Millicent gave birth to a baby daughter, Lisa, soon after. The child was taken away from Millicent though she was still given regular access. After three years under the care of mental health doctors, Millicent was deemed to be rehabilitated and released from detention. Disowned by her parents, Millicent Adams moved to build a new life on the West Coast.

Antonio Agostini

The case that became infamous as the "Pyjama Girl" murder was surrounded by mystery and took Australian police nearly 10 years to solve. The jealous husband, who eventually served time for Linda Agostini's death never fully revealed what happened that day, but it seems likely his passions were inflamed by her cheating and he set out to bring a murderous end to his unhappy marriage.

Italian immigrant **Antonio Agostini** married Linda Platt in 1930, and the couple settled in Melbourne, Australia. But their marriage wasn't a partnership of mutual support. Agostini worked at odd jobs to raise money, while Linda spent her days drinking and entertaining a string of lovers until suddenly, she disappeared. The last time anyone saw Linda Agostini alive was at her home in August 1934.

When asked about his missing wife, Agostini said that she had run away with one of her boyfriends, but before long a farmer discovered the body of a woman in a culvert between Melbourne and Sydney. She had been savagely beaten in her last moments before being shot through the head, then the corpse had been burned. Little was left to identify her from save the yellow silk pyjamas she had been wearing.

RIGHT: Linda Agostini was born in Forest Hill, London, in 1905. She moved to New Zealand at the age of 19 after a failed romance. In 1927, Platt moved on again to Sydney, Australia.

At first, police believed the body to be that of Mrs Anna Philomena Coots who had gone missing at the same time. Even Linda's mother could not confirm the mutilated body was that of her daughter but she wasn't told about the pyjamas that later proved to be a crucial piece of evidence. The case was closed and might have remained so were it not for a policeman whose wife had been a friend of Linda's. He was certain that the body was hers and set about trying to prove it. Finally, Linda's mother was shown a photograph of the pyjamas the murdered woman had been wearing and identified them as a set that she had given to Linda as a wedding gift. She also told police again that Agostini had mistreated her daughter. Linda was identified through dental records, and Agostini was arrested in 1944.

Under interrogation, he admitted to killing his wife 10 years earlier, but said it was not intentional. He told police that he and Linda had both got drunk on August 28, 1934, and that she had accused him of having an affair with a woman at the restaurant where he worked. Agostini said Linda had been drunkenly waving a gun around and when it went off by accident she had been shot. It was obviously a tissue of lies. Further examination of Linda's body revealed that her brutal head wounds had been inflicted before she was shot and that it one of these was that killed her, not a bullet. Incredibly, Agostini also maintained that he had no idea how her body had come to be burned and suggested that someone else must have stumbled across her corpse and set fire to it.

Agostini went on trial on June 9, 1944, charged with his wife's murder. But the charge was reduced to manslaughter, and he was sentenced to six years' hard labor. He was released in 1950 and returned to Italy.

Edward Charles Allaway

Edward Allaway had long shown all the symptoms of paranoia schizophrenia, but he was a quiet man who kept himself to himself and few suspected how deep his psychological problems ran except the women he was married to. But when his second wife left him, his weak grip on sanity broke and he went on a killing spree that left nine people dead.

Allaway was diagnosed as a paranoid schizophrenic during his first marriage to a woman named Carol and though he once received a month-long course of electric-shock therapy it did little to help. The delusions continued and were particularly vivid. Carol, he thought, was not only sleeping around but posing for pornographic photos behind his back. The fact that she remarried within days of the couple's divorce being finalized did nothing to stem his suspicions or alleviate his mental condition.

Nevertheless, Allaway married again within a few months of moving south to Orange County, California, in 1973, and he and his new wife Bonnie took a long, cross-country camping trip, living a hand-to-mouth existence and taking work wherever they could find it. Eventually, they returned to Orange County and Allaway's sister managed to secure her brother a custodial job in the library of California State University, Fullerton.

All of Allaway's old symptoms were by now beginning to re-assert themselves, and were chillingly similar to those he had had before. Like with his first marriage, Allaway was certain that Bonnie had begun sleeping with other men and also that she was appearing in pornographic films made by employees of the library where he worked. He also began verbally abusing his co-workers as well as becoming increasingly prejudiced toward African and Hispanic Americans. At home his violent streak became more pronounced. He was insanely jealous and threatened to slash Bonnie's face with a pen knife if he caught her cheating. It was more than she could bear. Bonnie left.

ABOVE: A memorial grove of seven pine trees that honors the seven people killed by Edward Allaway on July 12, 1976, in the library of California State University.

In a towering rage of jealousy, Allaway snapped. But where a more sane man might have tried to take revenge on his wife, he just wanted to inflict some of the pain he was feeling, indiscriminately. On July 12, 1976, 37-year-old Edward Allaway walked into the library at California State University armed with a .22 caliber rifle and fired. As he roamed the halls, the psychotic gunman shot nine people, killing seven. He then drove to the nearby hotel where his wife worked, called the police, and quietly surrendered.

In 1977, Allaway was convicted of murder, but found not guilty by reason of insanity. Although there was an attempt in 2001 to reintroduce him to society, it was overruled by a judge in 2003 who said that Allaway should not be released from the Patton State Hospital in San Bernardino County.

Henriette Caillaux

Henriette Caillaux was discovered by shocked staff at the busy office of Le Figaro newspaper in Paris standing over the dead body of her victim. The corpse of the paper's editor, Gaston Calmette, was riddled with bullets and in her hand Madame Caillaux held a smoking gun. Even so, Caillaux eventually walked free, having befuddled a jury with a mixture of psychology and pure theater.

While crimes of passion may occur in all societies around the world, the French seem to have a certain flair for them, and have even made laws governing how a *crime passionel* should be judged. Even so, the case of Henriette Caillaux was a complicated one. Although the victim of her murderous fury was an old lover, their affair had been over for years and would have remained forever buried if Henriette had not gone on to marry Joseph Caillaux, who would become the French Finance Minister. Her former beau, Calmette, meanwhile became editor of Le Figaro, one of France's leading newspapers.

Henriette's rage was sparked when Le Figaro began lampooning her husband in a series of article and cartoons published in the newspaper and reached boiling point when she and the Finance Minister were further humiliated. Calmette had kept some letters from his days as Henriette's swain and they included a love letter from Caillaux written to Henriette 13 years previously when she was also his mistress.

Wearing a fur coat over a gown and with her hands tucked in a muff Madame Caillaux arrived at Le Figaro's offices during the early evening of March 16, 1914. As the wife of the Finance Minister and a woman of some standing, she was immediately ushered in to see the Calmette. Standing before the editor, Henriette asked a single question: "You know why I have come?" Caillaux barely had time to answer "Not at all Madame", before his old flame pulled a gun from her muff and shot him six times. Newspaper staff immediately poured into the office and attempted to seize the murderer. With French haughtiness, Henriette Caillaux shouted "Do not touch me. I am a lady!"

RIGHT: Gaston Calmette, the editor of Le Figaro, who was shot and killed by Henriette Caillaux.

Today, the result of the trial would certainly be a forgone conclusion, and even then the future looked bleak for Henriette. But, as Calmette had already

discovered, she was a woman of considerable mettle who it was unwise to underestimate. French courts were notoriously sympathetic toward crimes of passion and she was determined to use that in her favor, even though she and Calmette had not been lovers for years. Appointing Fernand Labori, one of France's most

BELOW: Henriette Caillaux, in a photograph taken during the same year as her trial for the murder of Gaston Calmette.

celebrated lawyers, to defend her, Henriette Caillaux went into court with every possible argument prepared. The jury heard Labori criticize the 1804 Napoleonic Code that discriminated against women then argue that a woman must be expected to vent her passionate feelings.

Henriette herself performed amazingly on the witness stand, managing to present herself as a highly romantic woman at the mercy of her emotions while offering scientific research that showed how the nervous system and unconscious mind could make people capable of terrible actions under extreme pressure. Henriette's entire defense was intended to make her appear a heroine of uncontrollable passion to the jury, and a victim of psychological laws to the experts. In popular opinion women of ungovernable passions were to be viewed sympathetically—such strength of feeling was even desirable—while temporary insanity placed her beyond the law.

It worked like a charm. After a seven-day trial in the Cour d'Assises in Paris, Henriette Caillaux walked free. After less than an hour of deliberations, the all-male jury decided the homicide was committed without premeditation or criminal intent. The jurors accepted her testimony that when she pulled the trigger, she was a temporary victim of (as Labori put it) "unbridled female passions."

Yvonne Chevallier

The term *crime passionnel* could have been invented for Yvonne Chevallier. Hers was a rags-to-riches story that had all the ingredients for a fairy-tale ending, for it wasn't the money or respect that mattered to Yvonne; it was the dashing hero she had married. So when her adored husband became involved with another woman her life was shattered.

At 24 years old, Yvonne was working as a midwife at a hospital in Orleans, France. The daughter of a peasant family, she had little money and was uneducated, unworldly, and very shy—quite the opposite to the intelligent and ambitious doctor Pierre Chevallier, who was from an excellent family.

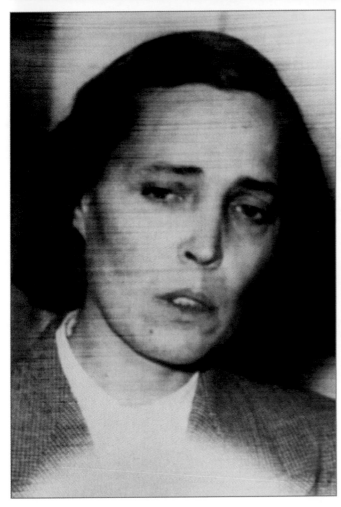

ABOVE: Yvonne Chevallier, pictured during her trial for the murder of her husband Pierre.

their free time was spent between the sheets. Chevalier's family strongly disapproved of the relationship with a mere peasant girl, but he ignored their protests. When war broke out in 1939 he became an even greater hero in Yvonne's eyes, and those of many others. He served as a medical officer with the French Army, saving lives at the front line. While on leave—and with none of Chevallier's family present—the passionate couple married in 1939.

When France was overrun by Germany a few months later, Chevallier became the head of the local Resistance movement. As the Germans retreated in 1944, Chevallier became an even greater hero. He led Resistance forces against the Germans and drove them from Orleans. On a wave of public acclaim Chevallier was elected mayor of the city the same year.

That was the first step on what would become a high-profile political career. As mayor, Chevallier organized the reconstruction of the city—a challenge that won him further praise when it was officially declared the best rebuilt city in France. He became parliamentary representative for Orleans in 1951, and from now on affairs of state would mean he spent much of his time in Paris.

Meanwhile, the sweet and shy Yvonne remained in the background. She bore Pierre two sons who became good friends with the children of wealthy neighbor Leon Perreau and his wife Jeanne. And while the children played, Yvonne became close to the couple, recognizing in them a pair who were as mismatched, but happy, as she and Chevallier. What Perreau lacked in physical attributes—he was short, fat and bald—he made up with his personal charm, and his success as owner of Orleans' most prestigious department stores, Jeanne was 15 years younger than her husband and a red-headed, spirited

Nevertheless, he was only two years older than her and the attraction between them was instant and intense.

Just a few weeks after they met, in 1937, she had moved into his apartment, where Chevalier's unquenchable desire for Yvonne meant that much of beauty who easily held her own in the political and social circles that made Yvonne feel so ill at ease.

Unfortunately, the state's affairs weren't the only ones that Pierre Chevallier was attending to. Ironically, unlike their both married couples, he and Jeanne were a perfect match and they were soon deeply infatuated with each other.

Even before she found out, Yvonne was displaying symptoms of a breakdown. Anxious over a husband who was so frequently far away, she smoked incessantly, drank endless cups of strong, black coffee, and was becoming increasingly reliant on the amphetamine and barbiturate drugs her doctor prescribed. It wasn't long before her intuition told her that her marriage had started to fall apart, and it was confirmed when one of her sons fell sick. She brought him into bed with her so that she could comfort him during the night, and Chevallier moved to a couch in his office. But when the boy recovered, her husband refused to move back into the marital bed. Where once he had been insatiable in his lust for Yvonne, now he would not touch her. She visited beauty salons and *haute couture* shops and even began trying to understand his political world in an attempt to win back his affections, but nothing worked. She was rejected and alone; her hero had now become her tormentor.

Her devastation became complete when she received an anonymous letter that explained her husband's new coldness. It told her that Chevallier was having an affair. This was confirmed when an increasingly distressed Yvonne discovered a letter

BELOW: Pierre Chevallier, in a photograph taken just a year before he was killed.

ABOVE: Yvonne Chevallier appearing in the dock at the Reims Court of Assizes charged with the murder of her husband Pierre.

was at first met with furious denials, then confession, and then a demand for a divorce so he could be free to marry Jeanne. Chevallier told his wife, "As far as I am concerned you are a free woman. Take a lover because I will never make love to you again."

In desperation, Yvonne turned to Leon Perreau, hoping with his help to break the lovers up. If the affair continued, she explained to him, she might kill herself from grief. Perreau's response was a shrug. He already knew about the affair and had accepted the humiliation of being a mari complaisant— compliant husband. Next, Yvonne visited the National Assembly to find her husband and beg him again to give Jeanne up. She was turned away, and Chevallier left to take a vacation with his lover, but not before telling his wife she was a "cow."

At first, Yvonne attempted suicide with poison, but it only made her ill. Then she obtained a firearms license and bought a Mab 7.65mm, a French-made semi-automatic with a nine-round magazine. It was the perfect weapon she later said, "to kill without any doubts."

On August 11, 1951, Pierre Chevallier returned to the family home to collect the last of his clothes and belongings. Imploring him to stay, Yvonne followed him to their sons' bedroom and watched as he kissed them both goodbye. The heartbreak of watching him say farewell to his children was overwhelming. Yvonne fell to her knees clutching at her husband's legs while he snarled at her to keep her hands off the Under Secretary of State. Then Yvonne ran to grab the gun she had bought earlier screaming that would shoot herself. Chevallier made an obscene gesture and sneered, "Do

in one of her husband's jackets. It was addressed to "Dear Pierre" and went on to say, "Without you, life would have no beauty or meaning for me." The note was signed "Jeanne." A confrontation with her husband it then. But only when I have left." They were the last words he ever spoke. Yvonne fired randomly at her husband, shooting him in the forehead, leg, chest, and face. He fell dead to the floor with Yvonne crouched over him. Only thoughts of her children prevented her from turning the gun on herself. As she stood up, the gun accidentally went off again sending a final bullet into Chevallier's back.

When the news of his murder at the hands of his wife became public the response was outrage. Although Yvonne knew what a vile man her husband had become, to the rest of France he was a revered politician and a national hero. So intense were emotions in Orleans that it was decided Yvonne's court hearing should take place some distance away, where passions were running slightly cooler.

However, by the time the trial began on November 5, 1952, the public's sympathy had started to come round to Yvonne. Tales of her husband's infidelity were well publicized and the frail and lost woman with her white face and gaunt appearance was a sight to melt the hardest of hearts. As one journalist would later write, "The French press went crazy, throwing caution to the wind with police reporters, court reporters, sob sisters, psychiatrists, novelists, the works. The French felt they invented the crime passionnel. They were determined to leave nothing unsaid and they left nothing unsaid. The whole country was outraged, or outraged that anyone would be outraged."

As each new detail of the case came to light support for Yvonne grew. By the time Jeanne Perreau came to give evidence she was hissed in court while confessing that her affair with Pierre Chevallier had gone on for five years. Her arrogant declaration that, "Love does not make one ashamed. I believe that for love one is never punished," caused such a stir that she was asked to leave. Leon Perreau, meanwhile, became a figure of contempt for his acceptance of his wife's infidelity. He even spoke calmly of how Pierre Chevallier was the favorite of all his wife's lovers and shared her bed on average three times a week.

When Yvonne herself took the stand public sympathy became total. After hearing of how deeply she had loved her husband and how she had fallen at his feet to try and prevent him leaving, only to receive a rude gesture in return, even the prosecuting counsel said that the death penalty in this case was not appropriate, calling instead for just a two-year prison sentence.

The jury took less than an hour to reach its verdict. Yvonne was acquitted. The Catholic Church later granted her absolution for the killing, but gentle, sensitive Yvonne could not absolve herself so easily. She took her sons to live in one of France's notorious mosquito-infested colonies in French Guiana, West Africa—a place that had once been a penal colony and was now described as a tropical hell. A desolate community of people still lived there and Yvonne returned to her work as a midwife among them.

Vincent Ciucci

Although 36-year-old Vincent Ciucci dreamed of a happy life with the woman he intended to marry, his existing wife and children stood in the way. However, he wasn't about to let his existing responsibilities scotch his dreams so he came up with a vile plan that would free him to begin afresh and also allow him to collect insurance money on his wife's death.

On December 5, 1953, Vincent Ciucci chloroformed his wife Anne and their three children and then shot each one in the head. He then set fire to his Chicago apartment behind the grocery store he owned to make it look like they had died in the flames. Thinking it would put him beyond suspicion, the grocer stayed in the house and when the fire department team arrived, Ciucci made a great show of stumbling out of the smoke-filled apartment, choking and begging for his family to be rescued. He had wrongly assumed that if their bodies were burned, the bullet wounds would be impossible to see.

It was a bungled attempt to disguise a murder. After they had retrieved the bodies, the police quickly realized that this was no ordinary house fire and took Ciucci in for questioning. He denied everything, saying '"I admit that I am a gambler and I like to fool around with women. But I wouldn't do anything like that. How could a man kill his own children? He would have to kill himself instead." Becoming more desperate he then concocted a story that mysterious intruders had entered his apartment and shot his family before putting a torch to the building. Incredibly, he claimed that he would not have heard the four shots because he was a heavy sleeper.

Ciucci was charged with the four murders and stood trial three times before he was finally brought to justice. At the first two, he was found guilty of first degree murder of his wife and two of their children. At the third he was also found guilty of the first degree murder of the third child. His defense counsel's pleas for clemency fell upon deaf ears, and Ciucci became the last man to die in the electric chair in Chicago on March 23, 1962. The execution took place at one minute past midnight and was witnessed by nearly 30 people including journalists.

William Corder

William Corder was more than happy to indulge in a sexual dalliance with Maria Marten, as others had done before him, but he hated the idea of marrying her. Instead, he arranged to elope with her, and when she met him on the night they planned to run away, he shot her.

The gruesome story of William Corder and Maria Marten would later become known as "The Red Barn Murder" and began in the little village of Polstead in Suffolk, England, in the early 19th century when she was 24 and he was just 22.

Maria already had two illegitimate children by former lovers by the time she and Corder, the son of a farmer, became involved and quickly became pregnant with another. With his attempts to keep their relationship secret now rendered useless by her swelling belly, Corder said he would marry her, but kept putting it off. When the baby died (amid rumors that it had been murdered), he decided that he no longer owed Maria the wedding she craved. Nevertheless, she continued to badger him.

In the late spring of 1827, after several more postponements on Corder's part, the couple arranged

RIGHT: An early-19th century illustration of William Corder, the perpetrator of the notorious "Red Barn Murder."

to meet at the Red Barn, close to Maria's house, so they could elope. Although there was no real reason for them to run away together, Corder claimed he had heard that the parish officers were going to prosecute Maria for having bastard children. Maria Marten was never seen alive again.

Corder disappeared from the village for a time, but later returned to say he and Maria were now happily living in Ipswich. He also said he could not yet bring her back as his wife for fear of the anger of his friends and relatives. Already though, the village folk were suspicious, and the pressure on Corder to produce his wife eventually forced him to leave the area again. Now he wrote letters to her family claiming they were living on the Isle of Wight, and gave various excuses for the fact that she had not contacted them.

Suspicion continued to grow, and on April 19, 1828, Maria's stepmother persuaded her husband to go to the Red Barn and dig in one of the grain storage bins. He quickly uncovered the remains of his daughter buried in a sack. Maria's body was badly decomposed but was identified, by her sister Ann, from her hair, clothing, and a missing tooth. Corder's green handkerchief was discovered around her neck. Although it was obvious that there had been foul play, it was difficult to establish the exact cause of Maria's death. It was initially thought that a sharp instrument—possibly Corder's short sword—had been plunged into her eye, but this wound could also have been caused by her father's spade when he was exhuming the body. The handkerchief at her throat suggested strangulation while other wounds suggested she had been shot.

Corder was tracked down to Brentford, Middlesex, where he was running a boarding house with a woman he had married. The police charged him with

BELOW: William Corder being executed at the gallows in Bury St. Edmunds, Suffolk, on August 11, 1828.

BELOW: A contemporary pamphlet containing details of the "horrid murder" of Maria Marten by her lover William Corder.

THE MURDER OF MARIA MARTEN

IN THE RED BARN AT POLSTED.

Containing the whole Account of the horrid Murder,

COMMITTED BY HER LOVER AND SEDUCER WILLIAM CORDER.

Which was revealed in a Dream by her Mother, and also a graphic

ACCOUNT OF HIS CONFESSION AND EXECUTION

R. MARCH & CO., ST. JAMES'S WALK, CLERKENWELL.

"murdering Maria Marten, by feloniously and willfully shooting her with a pistol through the body, and likewise stabbing her with a dagger." And in order to be sure of a conviction eight other charges were brought against Corder, including one of forgery.

Corder's trial started on August 7, 1828, at Shire Hall, Bury St. Edmunds. The court was so swamped with hopeful spectators that admittance was by ticket only. Finally standing before a judge, Corder pleaded not guilty to the murder of Maria Marten. He admitted being in the barn with Maria but said he had left after they argued. He claimed that while he was walking away he heard a shot, ran back to the barn, and found Maria dead with one of his pistols beside her.

It took the jury just 35 minutes to return with a guilty verdict. He was sentenced to hang and afterward be dissected. Corder spent the next three days in prison agonising over whether to confess to the crime and make a clean breast of his sins before God and after several meetings with the prison chaplain, entreaties from his wife, and pleas from both his warder and the governor of the prison, he finally gave a different story. While he still hotly denied stabbing Maria, he now said he had accidentally shot her in the eye as she changed into her traveling clothes.

Corder was hanged in Bury St. Edmunds on August 11, 1828, in front of a large crowd. One newspaper claimed there were 7,000 spectators, another as many as 20,000. His body was later used to demonstrate the workings of the nervous system to medical students.

Pauline Dubuisson

As little as she valued the faithful young man who adored her while they were together, Pauline Dubuisson was determined that he wouldn't find happiness. If she couldn't have him, then no-one could.

A young woman who was used to having everything she wanted, Pauline Dubuisson clearly didn't have much time for morality. During World War II, the young Frenchwoman had become the mistress of an enemy German Army officer when she was just 17 years old, and when she enrolled as a medical student at the French University of Lille after the war, she soon showed just as little regard for right and wrong.

At university in 1946, she met a charming and gentle-natured fellow student, Felix Bailly, and the two began a relationship. But during the stormy three years they were together, Pauline was anything but faithful. Smitten by his wild lover, Bailly proposed to her again and again and—just as frequently—Pauline turned him down and cheated on him.

Emotionally drained and heartsick, Bailly eventually came to the end of his tether. Leaving the wanton Pauline and Lille behind, he went to continue his studies in Paris where he soon met the beautiful Monique Lombard, a woman deserving of Bailly's love and who returned it fully. Finally happy, Bailly became engaged to Monique at the end of 1950.

Back in Lille, Pauline was furious when she heard the news. Although she had cared little for Bailly when she had the chance, she was the kind of woman who believed that she could treat men as her playthings and wasn't used to losing a lover to another woman. Her pride demanded that she win him back. But the tables were turned. The man who would have once done anything to win her love now rejected Pauline's advances, telling her that he was blissfully happy. His fiancée was the love of his life.

With venom in her heart, Pauline returned to Lille where she spent some money she had been given as a birthday gift on a .25 caliber automatic pistol. She then wrote a letter saying she intended to kill Bailly after which she would commit suicide. The note was soon found by Pauline's landlady who quickly sent a warning to Bailly. When Pauline arrived in Paris, Bailly refused to let her into his apartment, insisting that anything she wished to say to him could be said in public at a café. Having arranged a meeting, he duly arrived with a friend to protect him.

Pauline never turned up. But she was watching as he returned home. Soon after, Bailly answered a knock at his door, believing it to be another friend who was arriving to watch over him. Pauline raised the gun and fired three times. She then turned it upon herself and pulled the trigger. But the gun jammed. An attempt to gas herself also failed when a neighbor arrived to investigate the gun shots. Pauline was arrested and sent to jail to await trial. While there she would hear that the shame brought upon him by her actions had caused her father to write in sympathy to Bailly's family and then poison himself.

After attempting to slash her wrists the day before her trial began, Pauline Dubuisson was finally brought before a court in November 1952. Her lawyer attempted to soften the jury by using the old French defense that hers had been a crime passionnel. The jury found it unconvincing: her relationship with Bailly had ended 18 months before she murdered him. The suicide attempts were also seen as dramatic grabs at sympathy, and the court heard exactly how wayward Pauline's lifestyle was. She had kept a journal of all her lovers' performances, including Bailly's, and they were read out. When Monique Lombard took the stand, her good-nature and calm serenity left the jury with no doubt that the vicious and manipulative Pauline had been seething with rage at losing a lover to a woman so obviously superior to her.

Fortunately for her—and many said that it was more than she deserved—Pauline Dubuisson was found guilty of murder, but without premeditation. As a result, she escaped execution, but received a sentence of life imprisonment.

Frances Hall, Henry Carpender & Willie Stevens

It is most likely that this bloody and shocking double murder was instigated by a scorned wife who was all too aware that the infidelity of her minister husband was common knowledge. However, while some murderers successfully appeal to the sympathy of the court and others are set free through lack of evidence, Mrs Hall and her partners in crime appear to have spread enough confusion for the case against them to be completely botched.

The bodies of the Reverend Edward Wheeler Hall and his mistress, Mrs Eleanor Mills, were found laying side by side on September 16, 1922. She wore a red-spotted blue dress and black stockings as well as a blood soaked silk scarf around her neck. Her left hand rested on the knee of the Reverend Hall while his right arm was under her shoulder. Propped up against one of his shoes was a business card and all around were shreds of torn up letters. When pieced together one read: "Oh, honey. I am fiery today. Burning flaming love." Hall been shot once over the right ear. Eleanor had been shot three times in the right temple, under the right eye, and also over the right ear. In what could only have been a furious personal revenge, the choir singer's tongue had been cut out after she was shot and her larynx removed. It looked like a classic crime of passion.

Reverend Hall had been the pastor of the Episcopal Church of St. John the Evangelist in New Jersey; Eleanor Mills a singer in the church choir. Both were married. Hall's wife was Frances Noel Stevens, heiress to a sum from the Johnson & Johnson Company while Eleanor's husband James was sexton at St. John's. There were few people in the parish who didn't know about the affair. Hall and Eleanor had been involved for four years and a neighbor later told how the couple met every afternoon at Mills' house.

It was nothing out of the ordinary then, when Eleanor telephoned the Hall house on the evening of September 14. Both the maid and Mrs Hall herself would later testify that Eleanor had called the reverend about a medical bill, and that he had left the house on the pretext of discussing it with her shortly after.

However, it was no ordinary evening. After years of illicit meetings and secret passion Eleanor and Mills had finally decided to elope.

At the Mills' house, Eleanor told her husband that she was going to call Reverend Hall soon after dinner. When she returned she said that she was going to the church and there was a slight scene, during which she scornfully told Mills to follow her if he dared. It was the last time that Eleanor would be seen alive. The worried Mills waited until 11pm then went to look for her at the church. Finding nothing, he returned at 2am. Again, there was no sign of the lovers.

When he went to work at the church the next morning, he asked Mrs Hall if she thought their spouses had eloped. She told him that she thought they were dead. At around the same time, Mrs Hall's brother, Willie Stevens, told the maid, Louise Geist, that "something terrible" had happened during the night. Strangely, the bodies had yet to be discovered.

That changed the next day, and the police quickly took four suspects in for questioning: Frances Hall, Stevens, another of Frances' brothers named Henry (who was known to be an excellent marksman), and her cousin, Henry Carpender. Not long afterward, Hall, Carpender, and Willie Stevens were all charged with the murder of Reverend Hall and Eleanor.

The court hearing that followed was confused and mismanaged from the start and was eventually dropped for lack of evidence. But a few years later evidence that the defendants had perverted the course of justice began to emerge. In 1926, Geist's estranged husband claimed that his wife had received $5,000 from the Hall

family. He said that the maid had learned that Reverend Hall planned to elope and had forewarned his wife. The money was a payment to ensure her silence. Later, a state trooper who had been on the investigative team also claimed that Carpender had paid him to leave the state.

ABOVE: Two New Jersey State policemen (center), with two traffic policemen, waiting to escort a witness to The Hall-Mills Murder Trial, 1926.

A new court case also brought forward a compelling witness. Mrs Jane Gibson (also known as "The Pig

ABOVE: Willie Stevens on the witness stand during the trial in which he was jointly accused of the murder of Reverend Edward Hall and Eleanor Mills.

Woman," because she owned a pig farm) testified that she had witnessed the killings. She identified Carpender as the shooter, and told that he had been at the scene with Frances Hall and Willie Stevens. Gibson claimed to have returned to the bodies after the murder and had then seen Mrs Hall crying over her husband's dead body. Nevertheless, her testimony was ignored because she had given quite a different account in 1922. Despite a fingerprint on the business card left at the murder scene belonging to Willie Stevens, all three defendants were finally found not guilty on December 3, 1926. Some observers said the jury's verdict was a gesture of defiance to a Jersey City prosecution counsel who had called them "country bumpkins."

Gavin Hall

When hospital radiographer Gavin Hall found messages on his wife's computer that detailed a sordid affair it sent him into a catastrophic mental breakdown that ended in tragedy. But while his unfaithful wife escaped his murderous intentions, their three-year-old daughter did not.

One evening in October 2005, Gavin Hall's 31-year-old wife Joanne thoughtlessly forgot to switch off the computer. And when her husband came to look at it, the double life she had been leading was revealed before his disbelieving eyes.

Joanne had joined a sex contact web site for married people. A distraught Hall discovered that his wife saw herself as "an incredibly bored married woman" and "an easy lay." There were messages, too, from her lover; a 45-year-old married district judge called James Muir-Little. His profile said that he was a "38-year-old non-smoker" who had "a very active imagination and I think about sex all the time."

As Hall read the messages they had swapped, it became obvious that the pair were already involved in a highly sexual relationship. They had swapped naked photographs of themselves and described in graphic detail the sexual acts they would like to indulge in. The judge had also suggested setting up a sexual threesome.

When confronted, Joanne admitted the fling, but told Hall that it was over. She was lying. As her husband's mental state deteriorated she continued her liaison with Muir-Little all the while reassuring Hall that he had nothing to worry about.

Eventually, Hall's mental state had reached a point where he could no longer work, and he took sick leave due to personal problems. Now, he broke down completely. Suicide, he thought, was the only answer to his mental anguish and he also decided that his and Joanne's daughter Amelia—or Millie as the family called her—should die too. As he later explained to the court, the little girl had told him repeatedly that she wanted to "come with Daddy."

On November 29, 2005, Gavin Hall fed Amelia anti-depressant pills to make her drowsy. Father and daughter said farewell—"like Romeo and Juliet" as he later described it—before he smothered her with a rag soaked in chloroform.

Although Hall later told a court he had no memory of the night, he then sent lengthy text messages to his wife and her lover. One, sent to Joanne at 2.57am, said, "I loved you. Millie asked to stay with me. I've dealt with your deceit for two months, now you have the rest of your life to deal with the consequences." Shortly before 4am he again texted his wife. This time the message read, "Goodbye, Millie sends her love. She died at 3.32am. Love till death us do part I said and this is what I meant."

He then dosed himself with the chloroform and slashed his wrists. Millie died just two days before her fourth birthday. Her mother Joanne found her under a duvet on the living room floor that morning.

Hall's attempt at suicide was unsuccessful though. He was convicted of murder in November 2006 after a six-day trial and told by the judge he would serve a minimum of 15 years in prison.

Muhammed & Ahmed Hanif

The 14-year affair of Arshad Mahmood and Zahida Hanif might have gone on undetected for much longer had Arshad not decided to use his lover's passion for him to extort money from her. When her family found out, their revenge was terrible.

Doorman Arshad Mahmood's secret relationship with the married Zahida Hanif had begun in the early 1990s when he was in his late 20s. Although he was a cousin of her husband, Muhammed, for years the couple met for sex sessions without arousing suspicion until an argument over money started between Muhammed and his wife's lover. Arshad had recently helped Muhammed's younger brother Ahmed come to the United States from Pakistan, and thought he was owed $20,000 for his trouble. Muhammed disagreed. Arshad also disliked the fact that Ahmed was now living with the Hanifs, making meetings with his mistress more difficult. Blackmail, he decided, was the perfect answer to his problems.

During a particularly steamy session with Zahida, Arshad had filmed himself and his mistress making love. Now he threatened to show it to her husband if Zahida didn't give him the $20,000 he deserved and make sure that Ahmed was evicted. For months the petrified, unfaithful Zahida struggled to meet his demands, but eventually the strain became too much for her to bear. She broke down and confessed all to her husband.

Muhammed decided that rather than go to the police, the matter was best kept within the family and enlisted his young brother to help punish the blackmailing doorman.

The two men grabbed Arshad when he arrived at his cousin's home after work, smashed him in the face with a metal pipe and strangled him with their hands and scarves. They then put the body in Muhammed's car,

tearing his clothes, and removing all his possessions to make it look like a robbery, before dumping him on 54th Avenue near his Elmhurst home. Unfortunately for the killers, police found the explicit video in Arshad's work locker on June 9, 2005, and the whole case began to unravel. Muhammed and Ahmed were quickly arrested and charged with murder, though they appeared to have no remorse for their crime. A police spokesman later said, "They were kind of proud of it. They were joking around."

By the end of the month both men had been convicted and had begun their long sentences. Muhammed was found guilty of manslaughter and sentenced to 18 years in prison, while Ahmed got 21 years. At the trial, Robana Mahmood—Arshad's daughter—made it clear who she thought was to blame. Pointing to Zahida Hanif, she said "You all did it because she said so."

Jean Harris

When respected school principal Jean Harris met a man she liked and admired, murder was the last thing on her intelligent mind. But over years of betrayal and disappointment, love can turn even the most sensible of people into vengeful killers.

At 42, Jean Harris was a divorced and rather shy woman who was well-respected by her friends and colleagues at school. She was also not unusual in hoping that she might again find love in middle age, and at a dinner party in 1966 Jean thought she might have finally met a man who could make her happy. Dr. Herman Tarnower was a brilliant researcher at the Scarsdale Medical Center and would later earn himself a certain amount of fame on the publication of the successful book, The Scarsdale Diet. There was an instant chemistry between the pair and they began dating. Soon, Jean was deeply in love with Tarnower.

But he was not the type of man to be satisfied with a single lover, especially after he became something of a celebrity. Over the course of the 14-year relationship, he cheated again and again. Jean, who had never been

very confident, turned a blind eye while her self-esteem sank with every new revelation.

The situation came to a head in 1980 when Tarnower began a sexual liaison with Lynne Tryforos, who worked as a receptionist at the medical center. Jean feared that there was something between her long-term partner and the receptionist that went beyond his usual flings and became certain that she was about to lose Tarnower for good. On March 10, she wrote a ten-page letter to her lover, revealing all her insecurities and expressing her own self-loathing for having become so desperately needy. With the attention to detail that might be expected of a highly organized school principal she also finalized her will. Then she drove to Tarnower's home and would later claim that the gun she took with her was intended for her own suicide.

Jean said that she had fully expected her final pleas for love to be fruitless and wanted only to take her own life. But when she reached her lover's apartment the sight of Lynne Tryforos's lingerie in Tarnower's bedroom sent her into a rage and she shot her lover four times at point blank range.

Jean was arrested and charged with second degree murder. Released on $40,000 bail she then admitted herself to a psychiatric hospital. When her case came to court, on November 21, 1980, she pleaded not guilty to murder, insisting that the gun had gone off accidentally as Tarnower tried to wrestle it away from her. It was an obvious deception and courtroom observers at the time asked why her defense attorney had not pleaded that the murder was committed while Jean was in a state of

ABOVE: Jean Harris, photographed just hours before being found guilty of murdering her lover, Dr. Herman Tarnower.

extreme emotional disturbance with a view to her being convicted of the lesser charge of manslaughter. That, however, is exactly what her defense counsel had wanted. She refused.

After a 14-week trial, Jean was found guilty of murder and sent to the Bedford Hills Correctional Facility in Westchester County, New York, for the minimum of 15 years to life. Numerous appeals followed the conviction, but the higher courts all agreed that she had received a fair trial. She served 12 years of her sentence and was finally pardoned in December 1992.

Tony Mancini

In one of the most macabre murder cases of the early 20th century, petty criminal Tony Mancini was accused of killing his lover, Violet Kaye. But despite her decomposing remains being found in a chest that he had been using as a coffee table, Mancini was still acquitted. While there may be strong suspicions that the jury reached the wrong verdict in many other cases, in this one it is certain that they did. Years later, Mancini later made a deathbed confession.

The 42-year-old Violet and her 25-year-old lover inhabited a shady underworld of drugs, drink, and petty crime in Brighton, on Britain's south coast. She was a prostitute, and he worked occasionally as a waiter or at the door of a nightclub. Fuelled by their debilitating addictions and the difference in their ages, the couple's relationship was stormy, and jealousy boiled over on May 10, 1934. Violet had seen Mancini flirting with a teenage waitress at the Skylark Café, and witnesses later testified that an argument was already in progress by the time they returned to their lodgings.

That was the last time Violet would be seen alive. For nearly two months her body stayed in a trunk at the bottom of Mancini's bed. Although it smelled repulsive and fluids soon began to leak from it, Mancini simply threw a cloth over it and used it as a coffee table.

Meanwhile, he tried to cover his tracks by telling those who knew Violet that she had gone away for a while. He also sent a telegram to Violet's sister telling her the same. However, Violet's many prostitute friends became suspicious and reported her missing to the police. They immediately questioned Mancini, who panicked and went on the run. This was enough to prompt a police search and on July 18, they entered his lodgings. The first thing

LEFT: Violet Kaye, seen in a photograph from 1933, a year before her death.

that hit them was the smell, which led them straight to the grisly "coffee table" at the end of Mancini's bed.

The police eventually caught up with Mancini in London. He was arrested and faced a jury in December, 1934. Over the course of the five day trial the prosecution focused on the fact that Kaye had died from a fatal blow to the head and the gruesome coffee table Mancini kept at his lodgings. Who else but a murderer could live with a decaying body, they asked the jury. A handwriting expert was also brought in and confirmed the handwriting on the form for the telegram sent to Violet's sister matched that on menus Mancini had written at the Skylark Café. One witness, Doris Saville, said Mancini had asked her to provide a false alibi. Others—former friends of Mancini—claimed he boasted in the days after the murder of giving his "missus" the "biggest hiding of her life."

When the turn came for the case for the defense to be made, Mancini's counsel told the court of Violet's dubious drunken character, her jealousy, and—most crucially—her work as a prostitute. It was argued that Mancini had discovered her body at her flat and assumed she had been killed by a client. On the witness stand Mancini said he had panicked. He thought that because of his past criminal record the police would not believe his story and had put her body in a trunk then taken it with him when he moved to new lodgings.

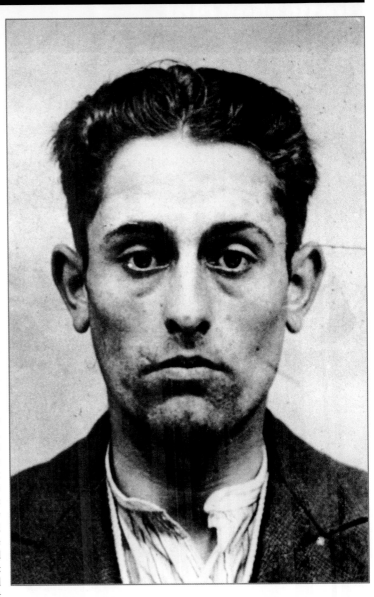

ABOVE: Tony Mancini, the petty criminal who only admitted to murder on his deathbed.

ABOVE: Tony Mancini leaving Lee Road Police Station, London, in a police car on the day of his arrest for the murder of Violet Kaye.

Slowly, the prosecution case began to fall apart. Blood-stained clothing that had been shown as evidence was proved to have been bought after Violet's death and the defense also told the jury that her body contained morphine. It was possible, they argued, that she had had fallen over while high on drugs and hit her head. In spite of their reputation as an argumentative couple, a number of witnesses also confirmed that Mancini and Violet had seemed contented. Mancini told the court he had loved his Violet even though she was a "loose woman."

After deliberating for two and quarter hours, the jury returned a verdict of not guilty and Tony Mancini

walked free. For the next 42 years though, his conscience plagued him, and in 1976, shortly before he died Mancini told a Sunday newspaper how Violet had died. During a blazing row she had attacked him with the hammer he used to break coal for the fire. He had wrestled it from her, but when she had demanded it back, he threw it at her, hitting her on the left temple and killing her.

Marie-Madeleine-Marguerite, Marquise de Brinvilliers

The eldest of five children, Marie-Madeleine-Marguerite was born into an aristocratic French family. Despite her nobility and good breeding, passion turned her into a monster; a serial murderer whose exploits would later inspired poet Robert Browning (*The Poisoner*) and several authors, including Alexandre Dumas (*The Marquise de Brinvilliers*) and Arthur Conan Doyle (*The Leather Funnel*).

The daughter of Viscount Antoine Dreux d'Aubray, a civil lieutenant of Paris, Marie-Madeleine-Marguerite submitted to an arranged marriage in 1651 at the age of 21. This was normal among the French aristocracy at the time, and the bride's her feelings on the matter were seldom taken into account. Unsurprisingly, Marie soon became deeply dissatisfied with her new husband, Antoine Gobelin de Brinvilliers. In addition to being a womanizer and gambler, de Brinvilliers all but ignored his wife, leaving her at the whim of temptation. It was close at hand: Chevalier Jean-Baptiste de Sainte-Croix was an army captain and friend of her father. The pair were soon locked in a passionate affair.

While her husband's illicit liaisons were well known in certain circles, her father was furious upon discovering his daughter was also having an affair. The fact that her lover was a family friend enraged him even further. Marie was forbidden to see her lover again, and in 1663 her father had Sainte-Croix thrown into to the Bastille prison in Paris.

Wrenched apart from the one man who had cared for her, Marie's passion turned to bitter hatred and a lust for revenge. When Sainte-Croix was eventually released, she ignored her father's order and was reunited with her lover. As chance would have it, he had learned the art of poisoning during his imprisonment. It was a skill the couple intended to make full use of as they plotted to take revenge on his lover's father, while at the same time ensuring Marie's inheritance. With the assistance of one of the royal apothecaries to the court of King Louis XIV, Sainte-Croix obtained tasteless but lethal potions, which Marie fed to her father. In 1666, he became her first victim.

Having killed once, it seems that Marie found it easy to do so again. Having quickly spent her way through her portion of her father's wealth, she turned her murderous attentions to the rest of her family. Her elder brother died in 1670, followed by her younger brother, and then her sister and sister-in-law. Of course, she also attempted to rid herself of an unwanted husband, but he proved stubbornly difficult to kill, though from now on he would be prone to mysterious illnesses.

Perhaps in an effort to find a potion that would finish him off, Marie worked to perfect her poison techniques on sick people in a local hospital. While visiting them under the pretext of being charitable, she killed as many as 50.

Her crimes were discovered in 1672. When Sainte-Croix died that year, his wife opened a box that he had told her was to be delivered, to his mistress. Inside were poisons and papers that made it clear the pair had been on a murder spree.

Marie immediately went on the run, but was arrested in Liege. Under interrogation, she threatened, "Half the people of quality are involved in this sort of thing, and I could ruin them if I were to talk." But whatever secrets she knew, Marie took them to her grave. The once haughty aristocrat was brutally tortured, her jailers mainly employing what was known as "the water cure," in which she was forced to drink 16 pints of water. But no further information was forthcoming. Tried in Paris in 1676, Marie was found guilty and executed, her body and severed head being thrown onto a fire.

RIGHT: Alexandre Dumas, whose *The Marquise de Brinvilliers* was inspired by the exploits of Marie-Madeleine-Marguerite.

Francesco Matta

First loves are notoriously difficult to forget. Those days of innocent youth coupled with the first stirrings of sexual excitement leave indelible memories and, sometimes, every relationship that comes after is compared to the one left behind. When Susan Matta stumbled across her first boyfriend on the internet site Friends Reunited all those old memories came flooding back and she again fell deeply in love. But the happiness she though she had found came at a price her husband was unwilling to pay.

Having been divorced, Susan thought she had finally found the man of her dreams when she met Italian Francesco Matta, who ran a successful restaurant in Devon, England, in 1999. Matta's own marriage had also been annulled, and the two wed in 2003, after which they moved to Matta's home town of Caligari,

Sardinia, to begin a new life running a business leasing villas to vacationers.

All was going well until Susan posted adverts for the couple's villas on the Friends Reunited site in 2004. They caught the eye of Stephen Keen who had been Susan's first boyfriend 35 years before when she was 14 and he was 16. He was now a flight lieutenant with the RAF and married with two children, but immediately contacted her. She was delighted to hear from her old flame and as email after email arrived in their inboxes they rediscovered their old bonds. When Keen's wife Doreen discovered what had been going on she wrote to Susan, demanding that she leave her husband alone, but it was too late: the couple had fallen in love.

In February 2006, Susan traveled back to Britain to see her long-lost love and by the end of the trip both were certain that they wanted to make up for all the lost years and live together on a permanent basis. In April that year, Susan wrote a letter to Matta telling him about Stephen. Her distraught husband called to beg her to return, but she simply kept repeating the words, "I'm so sorry."

Matta couldn't let go of the woman he loved though. As Susan and Keen set up home together in Tiverton, Devon, he sent a stream of text messages telling Susan how much he loved her and begging her to end the affair. And when his wife refused he eventually tracked down her new address.

On July 6, 2006, Matta arrived in Devon in a hired van. When Keen answered the door his lover's husband stormed in shouting, "I thought you were an officer and a gentleman." He then said he had a hired a mafia hit man to kill Keen, and that the couple would have to pay £50,000 for him to call him off. As Keen picked up the phone to call the police, Matta lunged at him with a knife, stabbing him four times in the throat. Susan cradled her lover as he lay dying on the floor.

BELOW: The Friends Reunited website where Susan Matta got back in touch with her first love, Stephen Keen.

When the police arrived Matta told them calmly, "I came here to kill the man. I have done what I had to do." Turning to Susan, he continued, "My life is over. Now you will suffer as I am suffering." And as he was led away, he told his wife "I love you."

Francesco Matta was tried for murder at Exeter Crown Court in October 2007. He pleaded not guilty. The jury heard that while he accepted that he had killed Stephen Keen, he felt he should be convicted of manslaughter on the grounds of diminished responsibility. After several days of deliberation, the jury failed to reach a majority verdict and a retrial was ordered. On April 18, 2008, the jury at a second trial had no such difficulties. They found him guilty of murder, and Matta was sentenced to serve a minimum of 11 years before being eligible for parole.

Florence Maybrick

The marriage of Virginian beauty Florence Elizabeth Chandler to British cotton broker James Maybrick would later become littered with betrayals and despair, but at first they seemed happy. Despite the 23 year difference in their ages—Maybrick was 42, Florence just 19—they married in London in July 1881, soon after meeting on the White Star liner *Baltic* during an Atlantic crossing.

The newlyweds split their time between homes in Virginia and the grand Battlecrease House in the Liverpool suburb of Airbrush and appeared to lead a happy life. The marriage was quickly blessed with a son, James, and after the couple settled permanently in Liverpool a daughter, Gladys Evelyn, followed. Meanwhile Maybrick and his vivacious young wife enjoyed a swirl of social engagements and mixed in the best society. Theirs seemed a perfect life.

But as is so often the case, behind closed doors the reality of their relationship was very different. Maybrick was a hypochondriac and had begun regularly taking the poison arsenic, the one cure he felt would relieve his imagined illnesses. And the trappings of wealth were not all they seemed, either. The couple had lived beyond their means and financial disaster loomed. In an effort to stave it off, Maybrick quietly made attempts to save money. Florence was given a small allowance on which she not only had to survive herself, but from which she was expected to pay the wages of five servants and all the household bills.

The marriage began to crack, but further humiliations were in store for Florence. The young wife, so pretty and spirited, now found out that her husband had been keeping a string of mistresses, one of whom had borne him five children. In those Victorian times there was little Florence could do except keep up the lie that all was well for friends and associates while fuming in private. Her perfect life of love and wealth lay in tatters.

The emotional strain must have been torture, as Florence tried to cope with an arsenic-addled, unstable, philandering husband under the threat of financial ruin. It is perhaps no great surprise then that when temptation arrived, Florence gave in quickly, seeking solace—and revenge—first in the arms of one her husband's brothers and then with a man named Alfred Brierley. The latter had been a guest at one of the Maybrick's popular dance evenings, which they continued to hold in order to keep up appearances. Florence became quickly besotted with him. Young, attractive, and healthy, Brierley was everything her husband was not.

Sad at home, and thinking herself deeply in love, Florence threw caution to the wind and booked a room at Flatman's Hotel in London under the name of Mr and Mrs Thomas Maybrick for herself and her new lover. Telling her husband that she was visiting a sick aunt for a few days, Florence joined Brierley at the hotel, and together they enjoyed several days of illicit pleasure. For the unfortunate Florence though, even this tryst was to be tainted with disaster and betrayal. Before they parted, Brierly confessed that he had fallen for another woman. As she later recalled, "He said he

BELOW: Liverpool cotton merchant James Maybrick, who died from arsenic poisoning.

could not marry me and that rather than face the disgrace of discovery he would blow his brains out. I then had such revulsion of feeling I said we must end our intimacy at once."

Meanwhile, in her eagerness to be with Brierly, Florence had forgotten that the hotel was a regular haunt of her husband's cotton-trading associates. It didn't take long for news of his wife's adultery to reach Maybrick's ears, and in those hypocritical times his fury wasn't lessened by guilt over his own frequent betrayals.

It seems that Florence soon got over her problem with Brierley. Soon after Maybrick saw his wife talking to her lover at the 1889 Grand National horse race at the Aintree course near Liverpool. And the romantic pair displayed every sign of be a happy couple. Humiliated and enraged, Maybrick tore into his wife when the couple returned home to Battlecrease House and a loud and violent row ensued. Maybrick punched his wife and ripped her dress. As she staggered away, he threatened divorce before storming out of the house—presumably into the arms of one of his mistresses.

Servants later reported that after the argument Florence appeared unusually calm. Serene even. One maid also recollected that it was at this time she had noticed that Mrs Maybrick had begun soaking large quantities of flypapers in arsenic in her room. These she had purchased during two visits to the local chemists. Florence

assured the maid that she had heard that the resulting mixture made an excellent treatment for the skin and ensured a pale complexion.

If Florence's mental state was already crumbling, the next calamity to befall her may have finally pushed her over the edge. She visited Brierley again, hoping to win back his affections after their tender moments at Aintree, but the young man told her that their affair was over for good.

James Maybrick became ill—quite genuinely this time—on the morning of April 27th – just over a month after his row with Florence. A Dr. Humphreys was quickly called to Battlecrease House, but could find no obvious cause for his patient's symptoms of

ABOVE: Portraits of Florence and James Maybrick taken from an 1889 edition of the British illustrated newspaper The Graphic.

vomiting, numbness in his limbs, and shivering. Vexed by Florence's revelation that her husband had been taking arsenic and strychnine and Maybrick's fevered denials, the doctor diagnosed chronic dyspepsia and left, hoping that this was just another instance of Maybrick's hypochondria.

Maybrick did not recover. Two days after the doctor's first visit Florence again bought flypapers at the local chemist, and soon after her husband's condition deteriorated. Still perplexed, Dr. Humphreys prescribed the Victorian cure-all tincture of white arsenic and carbonate of potash.

The previously popular Mrs Maybrick had by now become the subject of scandalous gossip. Word of the couple's sexually tangled lives had leaked out and it had become common knowledge that Florence was desperately unhappy in her marriage. The ever-fickle Brierley now also reappeared on the scene and, with neither he nor Florence making much effort at secrecy, it soon became widely believed that Florence was poisoning Maybrick in order to marry her young lover. Suspicions were further aroused when the Maybrick's nanny, Alice, intercepted a letter from Florence to her reinstated lover. Dated May 8, it read, "Dearest, since my return I have been nursing my M day and night. He is sick unto death."

The nanny passed the letter to Maybrick's brother Edwin, who in turn showed it to another brother, Michael. Together they rushed to Battlecrease House and promptly gave orders that Florence was not to be left alone in her husband's room. Nevertheless, her suspicious behavior continued. One servant later told police that Florence had been seen replacing the medicine in her husband's bottle with a different liquid, while another overheard Maybrick gasping out an accusation of poisoning to his wife.

James Maybrick died on May 11. The circumstances of his death were found to be suspicious and an immediate postmortem was called for. It revealed that Maybrick had been swallowing a particularly toxic irritant such as arsenic. On hearing the results, Florence fainted away and was taken to her own bed, where she would remain for several days, listening as the police searched her home for evidence of a crime.

They found letters from Brierley and enough arsenic to kill as many as 50 people. But what appeared to be an open and shut case was complicated by other evidence. Maybrick had been buying an arsenic-based tonic on a regular basis for 18 months and appeared to be long-term user. Nevertheless, Florence was arrested on suspicion of murder.

On July 31, 1889, she appeared at Liverpool Crown Court before Justice James Fitzjames Stephen charged with murder. Her defence put forward the argument that Maybrick's addiction to arsenic and other similar drugs meant that large traces of the poisons would be found in his body. Regular intake would have a cumulative affect, Florence's lawyers argued. Further, though Florence's marriage had been all but over, she had little motive for murdering her husband. The financial provision Maybrick had made for her and the children in his will was small, and Florence would have been better off legally separated from him.

It was undoubtedly a strong case, and perhaps that was just as Florence planned. However, it was not strong enough to convince the jury. In the end, it was Florence's last letter to her lover that condemned her. She had hinted that Maybrick would not live through his latest attack of illness, and it looked as though she was predicting his death with certain knowledge that it would soon arrive. It is also likely that Florence's adultery played a part in setting the disapproving Victorian jury against her.

Without her husband or her lover, who had fled to escape the scandal, Florence Maybrick was found guilty of murder on August 7, 1889, after the jury had deliberated for just 38 minutes. She was sentenced to death, and an execution set for August 26. However, many people in both Britain and America believed that the evidence against Florence was too slight to warrant capital punishment, and petitions flooded in. Just three days before Florence schedule's execution, news came from the Home Office that her sentence should be changed to life imprisonment. Her life may have been saved, but it was much less than a full pardon. The Home Secretary declared, "The evidence clearly establishes that Mrs Maybrick administered poison to her husband with intent to murder, but there is ground for reasonable doubt whether the arsenic so administered was in fact the cause of his death." His was to be the last word. No court of appeal existed at that time, and Florence Maybrick was taken down to serve 14 years in prison.

She was released in 1904 and returned to America where she wrote a book, *My Fifteen Lost Years*, and then became a recluse living in a remote cabin. She never saw her children again and died alone on October 23, 1941. Among her few possessions was a family Bible. Pressed between its pages was a scrap of paper bearing directions in faded ink of how soaking flypapers in certain substances made a useful beauty treatment.

Ruby McCollum

The murder of senator-elect Dr LeRoy Adams by African-American Ruby McCollum is not notable for being an out of the ordinary crime of passion. What makes it stomach-turning is the treatment that Ruby received purely because she was black.

Senator-elect Dr LeRoy Adams of Live Oak, Florida, was not a pleasant man. Although married, he kept a mistress and would later be revealed as a thief and fraudster. But one lover wasn't enough for him. Adams also forced his sexual attentions on Ruby McCollum, who was already a wife and mother.

Theirs was not so much an affair as an exercise of his power over her, and time and again she submitted to his sexual demands, eventually giving birth to a child she insisted was the doctor's.

When she fell pregnant for a second time, it tipped her over the edge. She asked Adams to arrange a termination, and he refused, telling her to keep the baby though offering no financial support. On the morning of August 3, 1952, Ruby shot and killed Adams at his office.

The jury at Ruby's trial was made up of white men and from the start it was obvious that she was not going to get a fair hearing. The court simply did not want to know about an African-American woman having an affair with a powerful married white man. Neither were they interested in the fact that she had begged him to arrange the abortion of their second child and been turned down. They also turned a deaf ear to the fact that Adams had another mistress. As far as they were concerned a black woman who killed a white man deserved the full penalty of the law, and the circumstances were irrelevant. Ruby was duly convicted of first degree murder on December 20, 1952, and sentenced to death.

Fortunately for her, the judge had made a significant mistake. He had not been present during the jury's inspection of the crime scene, and on July 20, 1954, the Florida Supreme Court declared the trial invalid and overturned Ruby's sentence.

At a retrial, Ruby pleaded insanity. Court-appointed physicians declared her mentally incompetent and she was incarcerated for 20 years in the Florida State Hospital for mental patients at Chattahoochee. She served the full term.

After her first conviction, Ruby's plight was followed in a series of articles written for the Pittsburgh Courier by journalist Zora Neale Hurston. Entitled *The Life Story of Ruby McCollum*, the pieces ran during the early months of 1953. They put forward the case that Ruby's trial sounded the death knell for "paramour rights" in the south of the United States. The presumed right of a white man to take a black woman as his concubine was finally at an end.

Ruby, the tragic victim of pre-civil rights America, died of a stroke on May 23, 1992, at the New Horizon Rehabilitation Center. She was 82.

Charlotte McHugh

Dull-witted, lazy, and promiscuous, Charlotte had the good fortune to marry a man who worked hard to keep her and their children. Sadly, she saw her hard-working husband only as a meal ticket and—when she fell in love with a romantic gypsy—the husband became an obstacle.

Charlotte McHugh was born in Ireland in the early 20th century and by the time she had grown in to a young woman it was obvious that she enjoyed flirting and tempting men far more than working. Nevertheless, her sexual allure snared her a husband; a soldier named Frederick Bryant. They married when he was 25, and she 19, and moved to the rural English county of Somerset in the early 1920s. There, Charlotte would eventually give birth to five children, though there were always doubts about how many Bryant had fathered. Even so, he did his best to house and feed his idle, cheating wife and the growing number of children that filled the house. In 1925, Bryant was given a job as a farm laborer in Over Compton, near Yeovil, Dorset. Along with a small wage, Bryant was also given use of a cottage as part of his earnings.

While her husband worked hard, Charlotte existed only for pleasure. Numerous men were only too pleased to satisfy her sexual cravings, and some of them were even tempted into her marital bed while Bryant was out in the fields. Among her lovers was a gypsy horse-dealer named Leonard Parsons to whom Charlotte was particularly attracted. On the pretext of earning a little extra money for the family, she installed him in the house as a lodger in 1933 and when he wasn't out on the open road or with his own wife and four children, the affair flourished.

Having gotten away with so much for so long, and now deeply infatuated with her gypsy lover, Charlotte threw caution to the winds. She now paraded Parsons around the local village on her arm as if he were her husband and not Bryant, and made no secret at all of her passionate, and carnal, love for him.

The conservative rural community was shocked. Charlotte's behavior cost her husband his job, and the couple were forced to leave their cottage and move to Coombe, near Sherbourne. Charlotte did not give up Parsons, however. She was determined to have him at any cost, and the best solution she could think of was to remove her husband from the scene permanently.

In May of 1935, Bryant became ill with stomach pains. The doctor did not suspect poison and diagnosed gastroenteritis and he recovered, only to fall ill again on December 11. He was obviously a sturdy man for once again he survived the poisoning. Eleven days later though his mysterious stomach pains returned, and this time Charlotte had upped the dose. Bryant became violently ill and died within hours. When his body was examined, four grains of undissolved arsenic were found in his stomach.

The police searched the Bryant's home where the ever-lazy Charlotte hadn't even bothered to conceal her crime properly. A tin that had contained arsenical weed killer was found in a pile of rubbish and traces of arsenic were discovered on shelves in the house and in one of her coat pockets.

Charlotte Bryant was arrested on February 10, 1936, and charged with the murder of her husband. Her trial opened at Dorset Assizes, Dorchester, in front of Mr Justice MacNaghten, on Wednesday May 27, 1936, and it was reported that the unintelligent Charlotte seemed barely able to follow the proceedings. During her defense she protested that she had been on very good terms with her husband, but numerous witnesses drew a more accurate picture of her marriage for the jury and on May 30, 1936, Charlotte was found guilty of murder and sentenced to hang. She was executed, aged just 33, at Exeter Prison on July 15.

Candy Montgomery

Candy Montgomery's savage axe attack on the wife of her former sex partner left two children motherless. There was no question that someone else might have committed the terrible crime; Candy admitted it, but the jury was convinced by her claims of a psychological disorder and, amazingly, she was allowed to walk free.

Unlike many people who find themselves caught up in extramarital affairs, Candy Montgomery was not swept off her feet in raw passion but deliberately set out to find a lover. The Texas housewife was bored with her husband of seven years and wanted some excitement. In her own words, she said she was looking for "fireworks'. The man she chose was computer software engineer Allan Gore whom Candy met at a church volleyball game. Soon afterward, she pulled Gore aside and asked him straight out if he was interested in having an affair. It would be dangerous as both Candy and Gore's families attended the same Methodist church , but the two reached an agreement: they would sleep with each other, but make sure not to fall in love. On December 12, 1978, Candy and Gore met for their first sexual encounter. It did not produce the fireworks that she had been hoping for and Gore, too, was unenthusiastic. They tried again on numerous occasions, but after 10 months the affair fizzled out.

On June 13, 1980, Gore kissed his wife Betty goodbye and left home for a business trip to Minnesota. Betty had their baby daughter, Bethany, at home, and their other child—six-year-old Alisa—stayed with the Montgomerys, with whose daughter, Jenny, she had become good friends. Gore spoke to Betty again just before his flight departed, but he became concerned when she failed to answer his frequent phone calls later that afternoon. He began phoning friends and neighbors, asking whether they had heard from Betty. One of them, Richard Parker, went to the door and called for Betty, but saw nothing. He told Gore that he had found nothing amiss.

Next, Gore called the Montgomery home to check on Alisa. Candy said she had visited the Gore's house at 10am during a quick break from Bible School. Betty was fine, Candy insisted. But by the evening, with his calls still going unanswered, Gore was becoming increasingly frantic. From his hotel room in St. Paul, he called neighbors again and pressed them to go inside.

Parker returned to the house with two other men. The front door was unlocked and, this time, they went inside. Parker immediately heard whimpers. He followed the sound and found little Bethany in a bedroom. The men then noticed crimson smears on an upright freezer in a utility room adjacent to the garage. They peeked around the corner, and there on the vinyl floor lay the body of Betty Gore. Her yellow top and pink shorts were soaked red, and blood had pooled and

congealed beneath her body. The men's attention was drawn to the right side of her face, which had been disfigured by what appeared to be a large gunshot exit wound. Her left eye stared blankly into the distance.

Almost immediately, the telephone began ringing. It was Gore. Parker gave him the bad news, saying, "The baby is fine. But Betty's dead. She's been shot. It looks a like a suicide."

It wasn't suicide, and it wasn't a gunshot wound either, as the police discovered. Under questioning, Gore at first denied ever cheating on his wife. Then he admitted his affair with Candy Montgomery, whose bloody fingerprint had been left at the murder scene. Candy was taken in and soon crumbled during interrogation. In her version of events Candy told detectives that Betty Gore had confronted her about her affair and on learning the truth had come at Candy with an axe. Candy was hit but not badly. She grabbed the axe from her friend's hands and in a blind frenzy swung it at Betty's face, not once but dozens of times.

During the trial, Candy's defense team told the jury that she suffered psychological problems that stemmed from a troubled childhood. It was also said that she had an aversion to blood, the sight of which brought on violent feelings. The defense's final argument was that Candy acted in self-defense when Betty attacked her. It was enough for the jury, if not for observers at the court. A verdict of not guilty was pronounced, and Candy was set free with cries of "murderer" ringing in her ears. A newspaper summed up popular feeling with the headline, "Woman Hacked 41 Times in Self-Defense, Jury Rules."

Alice & Thomas Morsby

Although she adopted the surname of her lover, Alice Morsby was actually the wife of Thomas Ardern, the mayor of Faversham, in the English county of Kent. In 1550, Arden was murdered by Alice who wanted to inherit his fortune and begin a new life with the man she adored.

The household arrangements of Thomas Ardern and his wife were more than a little unconventional for their time in Tudor England. That fact that Ardern had married Alice for her connections and money rather than love was not so remarkable, but he appears to have been either an unusually understanding man or totally in thrall to his tempestuous wife. He did not object when Alice took Thomas Morsby, a young tailor, to her bed and even appears to have been on excellent terms with his wife's lover. The mayor often invited Morsby to stay at the family home while he was away on business and enjoyed Morsby's company at the gaming table when he was at home. The official record of the case says that Alice "did not only keep Moresby carnally in her own house, but also fed him with delicate meats and sumptuous apparel, all which things Ardern did know well and willfully did permit."

Although she enjoyed the almost constant attentions of her lover, Alice was still dissatisfied. She objected to being one man's wife and another man's mistress. In 1550, after years of a dull marriage and desperate to be free of the husband whose very existence prevented her from marrying Moresby, Alice decided Ardern had to die. The first attempts of the fledgling murderess involved a poisoned crucifix and poisoned pictures. These weapons failed.

Next, Alice appealed to her lover for help. While Morsby refused to initiate the murder himself he gave in to Alice's demands and together they plotted Ardern's demise. Others were taken into their confidence: their servants Michael Saunderson and Elizabeth Stafford, Moresby's sister Cecily, and two men of the town, John Green and George Bradshaw. The latter was dispatched to Calais, France, with a mission to find willing assassins. He returned with two cut-throats called Loosebagg and Black Will.

As was their custom, Mayor Ardern and Thomas Morsby were sitting at the gaming table when the murderers struck. Black Will had been hidden in the house by Alice. The hired killer rushed into the room, threw a handkerchief around Ardern's neck, and strangled him. As the mayor's life faded, Morsby took up an iron and crushed his skull then brutally cut his love rival's throat.

The murderers, Moresby's sister, and the servants dragged the body to a nearby field. Black Will was paid the sum of eight pounds and immediately disappeared with his accomplice, Loosebagg. But the inept killers had failed to notice it was snowing and did not even bury the body. The next day Ardern's corpse was discovered, and investigators had no difficulty tracing footprints and bloodstains across the field back to the house. Everyone involved in the murder, with the exception of Loosebagg, who was never found, and John Green, were arrested, tried, and found guilty. Alice and her maid Elizabeth were burned alive at Canterbury on March 14, 1551. Morsby and his sister were hanged at Smithfield in London. George Bradshaw was hung in chains at Faversham. Black Will was burned on a scaffold. John Green was later apprehended in Cornwall and was returned to Faversham where he was also hanged in chains.

Augusta Nack and Martin Thorn

The 36-year-old Augusta Nack was an unlicensed midwife who also ran a boarding house—appropriately in Hell's Kitchen, New York City. A married woman, her husband had long since tired of her and after he departed Augusta took numerous lovers. The latest and most regular was German masseur Willie Guldensuppe, though when he went away on a trip, she could not resist the opportunity to introduce a little variety in her bed. Augusta decided that one of her lodgers, the youthful Martin Thorn, would suit her just fine.

Unfortunately for the couple, Guldensuppe returned unexpectedly in the middle of Augusta's seduction scene. Driven to a mad rage by seeing his lover in a state of undress and in the arms of another man, the German furiously attacked Thorn. Beaten half to death, the barber was hospitalized.

While he slowly recovered, Thorn's thoughts turned to revenge: On June 26, 1897, parts of Willie Guldensuppe began bobbing to the surface of New York's East River wrapped in distinctive red and gold

BELOW: William Randolph Hearst, the press magnate whose reporters helped to reveal the sordid details of the murder of Willie Guldensupper.

oilcloth decorated with flowers. His upper torso and arms were found in one part of the river, his lower torso in another, and his legs in yet another. The head, which—as the court later heard—had been coated in plaster, was missing. But as the coroners worked to piece the body together, they noticed another small part wasn't there: a four-inch square of skin had been cut from the corpse's chest. It would play a crucial part in identifying the body for investigations eventually led to the Turkish baths where Guldensuppe had worked, and his colleagues were able to identify the body from an abscess on one finger as well as telling investigators that the German had had a tattoo in exactly the place the flesh was missing.

Meanwhile, the press were covering the case avidly. Sensing a sensational story, the newspaper magnate William Randolph Hearst assigned a large group of reporters from his Journal newspaper to the case, and soon they were making breakthroughs. First, they found Augusta, who oozed guilt when the pack of reporters quizzed her. She had withdrawn a large amount of cash from her bank account and had made enquiries about leaving for Europe on a steamship. The journalists also discovered where the oilskin had been bought, and by whom. Thorn was arrested soon afterward as he tried to slip across the border into Canada.

While Thorn denied everything, Augusta confessed under questioning. She told police that she had become tired of her German lover's numerous affairs while demanding that she remain faithful and that she had lured Guldensuppe to a farm cottage on the promise of sex. It was there that Thorn had taken his own bloody revenge. Hearst's reporters soon tracked down the Long Island farm where the owner said a couple matching Thorn and Augusta's description had rented a cabin.

The farmer said he had noticed how all his ducks had suddenly turned pink while they had stayed there! They had been bathing in wastewater flowing from a pipe connected to the cottage. It was later discovered that Thorn had shot Guldensuppe, stabbed him, and cut him up in the bathtub.

So graphic were the details of the murder that during the trial a sensitive juror fainted. Augusta and her young lover were both convicted of murder, but while Augusta was sentenced to 15 years (serving nine) in Auburn Prison, Thorn met his death in the electric chair on August 1, 1898, at Sing Sing.

Fernado Ortega

A short and simple story, the case of Fernado Ortega perfectly captures the despair that accompanies humiliation and rejection. His was a sad, but typical, crime of passion.

Garage owner Fernado Ortega of Guadalajara, Mexico, knew he could never have the woman he desired. She was beautiful, while he was hunchbacked and ugly. They met in 1972 when Maria Pineda became Ortega's nurse, administering injections and generally caring for her patient who suffered from chronic tuberculosis alongside his physical deformity. And as the weeks passed Ortega's attraction to the pretty woman grew into an love.

That Maria did not return his feelings was obvious, but still he tried to explain how he felt. When she rejected him, Ortega's love turned to despair and desolation at his own physical shortcomings. Perhaps we could have felt pity for him, but for the fact that Ortega decided that if he could not have Maria then he could not bear for her to be happy with anyone else. At knifepoint he forced her to drink deadly cyanide and laid her expiring body on his bed. As she lay dying, Ortega then he drank from the bottle himself and lay down beside her to await death.

The horrific scene was discovered by Francisco Pineda, a car mechanic who worked for Ortega and who—tragically—was also Maria's stepfather. His first thought was that Ortega had overpowered her so that he might rape her, but though Maria's skirt had slipped up to her thighs, Ortega had not wanted to violate the woman he loved. There was no sign that he had sexually abused her at all.

Pauline Yvonne Parker & Juliet Marion Hulme

The case of two teenage lesbian lovers who murdered one of their parents shocked New Zealand in the mid-1950s. The two girls were so desperate not to be parted from one another that they were prepared to kill to stop it happening.

ABOVE: Juliet Marion Hulme (left) and her friend Pauline Yvonne Parker after being remanded in custody charged with the murder of Pauline's mother Honara Mary Parker.

Pauline Parker and Juliet Hulme came from different worlds. Pauline's father managed a fish shop while her mother, Honora Mary Parker, took in lodgers to make ends meet; Juliet's father was a famous British physicist and her mother a marriage counselor. Nevertheless, the two young girls were drawn to each other, perhaps due to their similarities in temperament. Pauline's education had not been of the highest standard, but she was a gifted and imaginative writer, and Juliet was deeply sensitive to the point of being psychologically fragile.

Over time, what started out as a friendship became much, much more. The two adolescent girls—Pauline was 15, Juliet 16—began to explore their sexuality with one another and quickly became passionate lovers. As Juliet would later say, when they were together it was "better than heaven." Unfortunately, events were conspiring to bring their relationship to an end. Juliet's marriage-counselor mother divorced her father, and the young girl was deeply traumatized when she caught her mother in bed with a new man. Soon after, her father announced that he was returning to Britain to take up a new post, and Juliet would be sent to live with relatives in South Africa where it was hoped her health would improve.

Both girls were devastated at the idea of being separated, but Honora Parker made no secret of her relief. She had grown suspicious of their friendship and the strange hold Juliet had over her daughter, so when Pauline begged to be allowed to go to South Africa too, she refused. In doing so she became the focus of the girls' frustration and anger. If Pauline was orphaned, they reasoned, there would be no-one to stop her joining Juliet in South Africa. As Pauline wrote in her diary on February 13, 1954, "Why could mother not die? Dozens of people are dying, thousands are dying every day. So why not mother and father too?" It would be one of the many diary entries that eventually helped convict her.

On June 22, not long before Juliet was due to leave, Honora Parker took the two girls to Victoria Park for tea and cakes. After the treat, the three strolled in the park and when they reached a secluded spot, Mrs Parker bent over to pick up a stone that had attracted her attention. As she did a stocking loaded with a brick crashed into her skull. Over and over, the teenage girls took it in turns to beat Pauline's mother to death. And when they were sure that she was gone, they ran back to the tea kiosk, screaming for help and crying, "Mummy's been hurt."

Police found the stocking and brick close by Honora Parker's body and the two girls were arrested. Both admitted that they had they had helped in the grisly task of killing Mrs Parker, and both were found equally responsible. After a sensational trial unlike any New Zealand had ever seen, the two girls were found guilty of murder on August 29, 1954, and—in view of their ages—sentenced to five years in prison each with the added condition that when they were released they could never see each other again.

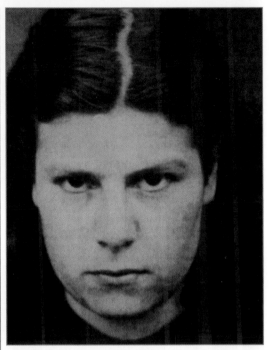

ABOVE: A New Zealand police mug shot of Pauline Parker, who was convicted with her best friend Juliet Hulme for the murder of her mother in 1954.

Alpna Patel

When Alpna Patel was married to a man she hardly knew, she didn't realize that along with a husband she would be getting a father-in-law who wanted to control every detail of her life. When she was forced to sleep in his basement while her new husband worked 500 miles away, she became desperate to get out of her appalling situation.

Alpna was 29 and her soon-to-be husband 26 when their marriage was arranged for them in 1998. Although they were both American, their families stuck rigidly to the rules of their homeland's culture and during the "courtship" the couple were strictly chaperoned during meetings and the brief dates they were allowed. The traditional wedding was an extravagant affair and afterward the couple, finally alone together, went to Disneyworld to enjoy a honeymoon during which they could get to know each other. As

LEFT: This wedding photo of Alpna Patel with her husband Viresh Patel was introduced as evidence during her trial for his murder.

Viresh Patel would now begin to discover, his new wife had a reputation for being "moody" and "temperamental."

It didn't take long for the marriage to begin to disintegrate. Back home from their brief vacation, Alpna found that her new father-in-law had strong ideas about how the young couple's lives should be run and as head of the family he was determined to implement them. Alpna was allowed to continue her work as a dentist at a local hospital in Buffalo, New York, but was told she had to live in the basement of her in-laws house and now needed to submit to her father-in-law's will in all aspects of her life. She even needed to seek his permission before going out with friends. Her husband, meanwhile, was to continue as a surgical resident in Baltimore, where he had an apartment that would become their married home on the occasions they spent time together.

For Alpna, the situation was intolerable and in March 1999, it came to a head. When her husband made a brief appearance at his parents' house, Alpna confronted him and a vicious argument was overheard by Viresh's sister. A day later a scowling Alpna argued with him again in the driveway. On March 23, 1999, Alpna Patel dropped another sister-in-law, Beena, off at school. As a court would later hear she seemed in a good mood and was even "giggly." She made no mentions of her plans for the rest of the day, but after Beena was delivered to school, she drove to the airport and took a plane to Baltimore.

When Baltimore police arrived at the Patels' one bedroom apartment the next day, they found Alpna sitting at the kitchen table—she was covered in blood. In the bedroom was the body of her husband, his jugular and carotid artery slashed with a knife that had been part of a set given to the couple as a wedding gift.

In court Alpna Patel claimed the killing had been self defense, stating that she and her husband had discussed the problems with their marriage, after which they had decided to sleep on it. She had awoken two hours later to find Viresh straddling her and pointing a black-handled steak knife at her chest. She told the court that she had managed to knock him off her and in the ensuing struggle for the knife, her husband was killed.

Alpna was acquitted of first degree murder at her first trial and the jury could not agree on the charge of second degree murder. At a second trial, in September 2000 she was given a three-year sentence for manslaughter. She served 13 months and was given credit for three more spent in custody during the trial. She was released in February 2002.

BELOW: A photo of Alpna Patel, 26, taken by Baltimore police after she was brought to the police station for questioning in connection with the murder of her husband.

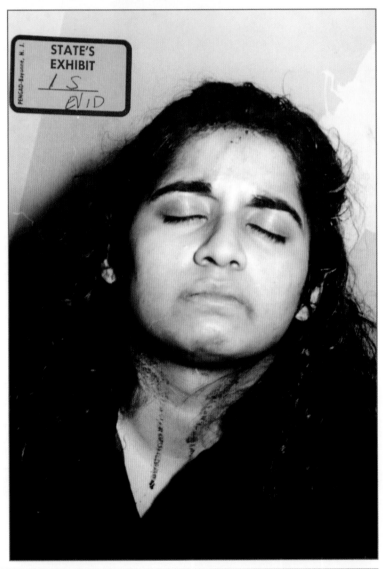

ABOVE: Alpna Patel (right) with assistant attorney Lynn Williamson walking from court in Baltimore, during her trial.

Nan Patterson

Sex, adultery, and blackmail—the sensational 1905 murder trials of the beautiful young dancer and performer Nan Patterson had it all. And though the evidence against her was overwhelming, still she walked free, saved from the death penalty by her looks and an air of innocence that came easily to a professional actress.

The wealthy bookmaker Caesar Young died of a gunshot wound in the back of a horse-drawn hansom cab on the way to meet his wife at the New York docks where the couple were due to take a ship, bound for an extended tour of Europe. With him was another passenger; Nan Patterson, a young actress with whom Young had been conducting an illicit two-year affair. The lovers had met to say their farewells before

Young's departure. They had also marked the occasion with a drinking spree.

As the only other person in the cab, Nan was arrested immediately, and it looked to prosecutors like an open and shut case. But when the case came to court and the details of the affair began trickling out, the press went wild and public support quickly surged around the actress. Nan Patterson, it was reported, had met Young two years earlier on a train to California. Despite her youth she was already married, as was he, but Nan was dazzled by the rich older man and the pair embarked on a passionate affair. As time went on Young gave Nan the money to divorce her husband, promising that he, too, would soon split from his wife. While she waited, he lavished his young mistress with expensive gifts and money. As is so often the case though, Young's divorce never materialized, and documentary evidence was produced that showed Nan had recently begun trying to blackmail her sugar daddy. Matters had come to a head in the back of the cab, and ended with Young slumped dead in his seat.

Nan denied all charges, testifying that Young had killed himself because she had ended their relationship, but the evidence continued to mount. The jury heard that on the day of Young's death, Nan's brother had pawned jewelry and used the cash to buy a gun. Still, the actress protested her innocence. The trial ended with a hung jury.

A second trial was convened with the press again feeding an insatiable public hunger for every tiny detail. The sheer volume of sympathetic, colorful newspaper articles meant that the public remained staunchly on the side of the accused. Nan maintained her plea of not guilty and she and her defense team played on her youth and saintly appearance for all it was worth. Her lawyer at one point declared, "What is there against this girl? She went on the stage, but it was to make an honest living. She met Young when she was but 19 years old. Who was the stronger of the pair?" When the trial ended, the New York Times reported that the closing scenes were "arousing public interest to a degree almost unprecedented in the history of criminal cases in New York."

The trial ended on June 3, 1905, with another hung jury unable to agree a verdict. Nan Patterson spent nearly a year in jail while legal discussions rambled on and talk of a third trial fizzled out. In the end it was felt that in another trial, any jury would base its decision on newspaper reports even though the evidence against her was so strong. Eventually, a court set her free. Nan walked out of the building to be welcomed by a cheering throng of supporters.

Queen Elizabeth I & Sir Robert Dudley

Queen Elizabeth I never married and is remembered by history as the Virgin Queen—the root of the name Virginia, which was named in her honor. However, the reality was very different. Although it remains unproven, the Queen is thought to have taken Sir Robert Dudley as a lover and conspired with him to murder his wife. The evidence against them is circumstantial but compelling.

Queen Elizabeth I never married and is remembered by history as the Virgin Queen—the root of the name Virginia, which was named in her honor. However, the reality was very different. Although it remains unproven, the Queen is thought to have taken Sir Robert Dudley as a lover and conspired with him to murder his wife. The evidence against them is circumstantial but compelling.

ABOVE: An 1879 painting by William Frederick Yeames depicting the death of Amy Robsart.

It is beyond doubt that Sir Robert Dudley was a philanderer and fiercely ambitious, yet his love for Queen Elizabeth appears to have been genuine. He was her constant companion and confidant for more than 30 years. After the death of his wife, Amy Robsart, he turned down numerous offers of marriage, including to a number of foreign princesses and one to Mary, Queen of Scots, which could have placed him on the thrones of both England and Scotland. All this he sacrificed in order to remain by his queen's side. For her part, Elizabeth heaped honors and riches upon her favorite companion. Indeed, the court of the day was inflamed with gossip regarding the pair, and it was widely believed that there was an love affair between them and that they would be married if and when Amy died.

Amy was the fly in the ointment of the Dudley's love for the queen. Although theirs appears to have been a love match, made when Amy was just 18, Dudley and his wife had been leading separate lives since Elizabeth I had come to the throne, and Dudley began to spend more time at court.

On September 4, 1560, the Queen had a strange—and rather suspicious—conversation with the Spanish ambassador during which she said that Amy Robsart was "dead or nearly so." In fact, it was widely known that Amy had a "malady in one of her breasts," which was possibly cancer. Nevertheless, it is suspicious that only four days later Amy was indeed dead. On September 8, she allowed all

her servants to take the day off to go to Abingdon Fair in Oxfordshire. When they returned, they found her at the foot of the stairs with a fractured skull.

While her death was officially deemed to have been a tragic accident, whispers soon circulated. There was a belief that Dudley and the Queen had organized Amy's murder between them; a belief that was strengthened when one of Dudley's staff was reported to have been part of the plot. It is possible, however, that such rumors were started for political reasons. There were some members of the royal court whose interests would have damaged by a marriage between Dudley and the queen. If so, the rumor-mongers won the day. Perhaps fearing to further inflame the scandal, Elizabeth and Dudley never married.

LEFT: A painting of Queen Elizabeth I of England by Flemish artist Steven van der Meulen.

RIGHT: A picture of Robert Dudley, Earl of Leicester, from around the time of Amy Robsart's suspicious death.

James Stewart Ramage

Fearing a violent reaction from a husband who had a history of lashing out when crossed, Julie Ramage made a careful plan to leave him as gently as possible, but she was only delaying the inevitable. Fourteen months later he took her body out to Australia's Kings Lake National Park and buried it.

To all appearances **James and Julie Ramage** had a perfectly normal middle-class family life. They owned a beautiful home in Melbourne, Australia, as well as a holiday house and the three cars in the garage, and had a very healthy bank balance. But Julie lived in fear of her 43-year-old husband and told friends that he might "lose it" one day. Nevertheless, keen to provide a stable family environment for their children, she endured his temper and occasional outbursts of violence for 20 years before finally deciding to leave.

In order to let him down gently Julie enlisted the help of friends and family. Avoiding a face-to-face confrontation, she left the family home while he was on a business trip abroad, leaving him with a letter that suggested they might get back together after a while. As she explained to friends, he was not ready to face the truth. The letter was a moving appeal for peace between them. She wrote, "If you do care for me, please let me go without a horrible fight, for the kids' sake. Let's prove to them that we are better than all the other separated couples that we know. I could hate you so much for some of the things you have done and said to me over the years, but I also understand that you are a good person and that you work hard and, most importantly, that you love our kids very much."

However, Julie had no intention of ever going back to her husband and before long had met a new man, Laurence Webb. Meanwhile, James Ramage seethed with anger at the desertion. On July 21, 2003, the violent confrontation that Julie had worked so hard to avoid exploded. Having regained her confidence and made furious during and argument, Julie told her husband that sex with him had repulsed her and that she should have left him 10 years earlier.

Ramage's response was terrible. He strangled his wife then put her body in his car, packed a change of clothes, and gathered up Julie's handbag and mobile. He then drove out to Kings Lake National Park and on the way called his wife's work and mobile numbers as if he were looking for her. At the park Ramage dug a hole and put Julie's body in it, then covered the newly turned soil with branches and bracken. A few meters away he dug a second hole, where he buried incriminating evidence, including the bedding that he had used to wrap her body.

Julie's disappearance didn't go unnoticed for long, and Ramage's long history of violence and the calls he had made after killing his wife immediately brought him under suspicion. Nevertheless, at his trial—which began on December 9, 2004, at Victoria's Supreme Court—he made full use of Julie's own outburst of temper to claim that he had been provoked. Although the prosecution argued that she would have been too afraid of Ramage to actually speak to him in that way, after 20 years of taking his verbal and physical abuse, Julie's alleged final snap of anger at her husband saved him from a murder charge. The jury found that he should be convicted of manslaughter. The judge, however, did not appear to be quite so convinced. Sentencing Ramage to a maximum 11 years in prison, Justice Robert Osborn said, "The killing was done with murderous intent and savage brutality and where, although the jury has accepted the reasonable possibility of provocation, it is apparent that such provocation was not objectively extreme."

Julie Ramage's mother, Patricia Garrett, perhaps summed it up best. Describing her son-in-law's prison sentence as pathetic, she said, "Any woman that's in a relationship where she feels threatened, I tell her not to stay for the sake of the children. Get out. My daughter stayed for the children, and she's paid the ultimate price. She's dead."

Dr. Buck Ruxton

The murder of Isabella Ruxton at the hands of her common-law husband was a classic crime of passion. Incensed at her cheating on him, Ruxton strangled and stabbed his wife to death, then turned his killing fury on a maid who had the misfortune to walk in and witness the act. The only thing missing was Isabella's guilt, for she was a faithful wife and completely innocent of the accusations he made against her.

A doctor of Persian ancestry, Buck Ruxton's jealousy of his wife was common knowledge among their circle of friend and acquaintances in Lancaster, England. In fact, he had become so suspicious of Isabella that when she took a trip to Edinburgh with some friends he secretly followed her, certain that she

ABOVE: Dr Buck Ruxton, who was convicted of the murder of his wife, Isabella Ruxton, and his housemaid, Mary Jane Rogerson at his home in Lancaster.

passion that violence took possession of him. He grabbed at his wife, strangled her into unconsciousness, and then stabbed her to death. During the struggle a maid, Mary Rogerson, heard Isabella's screams for help and she rushed to help, only to find Ruxton standing over the body of his wife. He immediately knew that if he were to escape punishment then Mary would have to die too and he quickly dispatched her in the same way. Then, Dr Ruxton set about concealing his crime. First he had to deal with the bodies. On September 15, 1935, two severed heads and assorted dismembered limbs were found wrapped up in copies of the Sunday Graphic newspaper.

When Mary Rogerson's parents asked after her, Ruxton told them that their rather plain and single daughter had fallen pregnant and his wife had taken her away to have an abortion. They didn't believe him and reported her missing. Meanwhile, friends and neighbors had also begun to question why Isabella Ruxton had suddenly vanished. Ruxton was well known for his temper and jealousy and the rumor that he was responsible for the killings spread like wildfire. In desperation, and eager to throw detectives off his scent, Ruxton presented himself at the police station and begged for their help in finding his wife.

Unfortunately for Ruxton, he was already the prime suspect. The new forensic sciences of fingerprinting and super-imposure (where a photograph of a victim is matched to a skull) had allowed police to identify the victims, now all they needed was the evidence to convict Ruxton. They found it in the testimony of Ruxton's cleaner, who told them that on the day the two women went missing she had arrived at the house to find it in disarray with blood-stained carpets.

Ruxton was arrested on October 13, 1935, and tried at Manchester Assizes in March 1936. The jury took just over an hour to find him guilty of murder. Although a petition to have his sentence commuted was signed by 10,000 people it failed and he was hanged at Strangeways Prison in Manchester, on May 12, 1936. A few days later his signed confession was published. It read, "I killed Mrs. Ruxton in a fit of temper because I thought she had been with a man. I was mad at the time. Mary Rogerson was present at the time. I had to kill her."

was having an affair with a man called Robert Edmonson who was among the group. But while his snooping didn't turn up a single scrap of evidence against her, the facts did nothing to quench the fury that was boiling within him as he followed his wife from one hotel to another, sure that she was sharing Edmonson's bed.

Isabella returned home to find her husband waiting for her. By now he had worked himself into such a

O. J. Simpson

It was the trial of the century, possibly the most famous and widely followed courtroom drama ever witnessed. And at first it seemed an open and shut case: the celebrity suspect had been watched on televisions around the world apparently fleeing justice, motive was clear, and crucial evidence had been found in the shape of an incriminating glove. All the elements of an obvious crime of passion were in place. And yet the former football star, O. J. Simpson was acquitted of the charge of murdering his ex-wife Nicole Brown Simpson and her friend Ronald Goldman. He walked free in 1995 after the longest trial in Californian history.

The drama began at 11.40pm on June 12, 1994. The barking of Nicole Simpson's pet dog alerted neighbors that something was amiss and the police were called to her Brentwood, Los Angeles, home. What they found there was truly shocking. While her two young children— Sydney, 8, and Justin, 5—slept upstairs, Nicole and her friend Ronald Goldman had been brutally slain. Nicole had been stabbed many times through the throat; the wounds so ferocious she was almost decapitated. Goldman had minor wounds to his body as well as fatal slashes, suggesting the murderer had played with his or her victim before finally despatching him. The police put the time of the double murder at between 10.15 and 10.40pm.

It did not take long for investigators to name Nicole's ex-husband, the football star O. J. Simpson, as the prime suspect, and an appeal went out for him to turn himself in while a huge crowd of reporters gathered at the police station. Instead, Simpson responded by sending a letter, which his lawyer read out. It said, "First everyone understand I had nothing to do with Nicole's murder... Don't feel sorry for me. I've had a great life." It followed by naming Simpson's partner at the time Playboy Playmate Traci Adell as an alibi.

The hunt was on. Police tracked calls from a cell phone in Simpson's van in Orange County and, later, a patrol car spotted a white Ford Bronco being driven by Simpson's friend, Al Cowlings, headed south on Interstate 405. Cowlings yelled that Simpson was pointing a gun at his own head. The officer kept his

RIGHT: O. J. Simpson accompanying his children, Sydney and Justin, at the funeral service for his ex-wife, Nicole Simpson.

ABOVE: Police cars pursuing the Ford Bronco (white, right) driven by Al Cowlings, carrying fugitive murder suspect O. J. Simpson.

distance, but followed the vehicle, which was traveling at just 35 miles an hour. For some time a Los Angeles KCBS News Service helicopter had exclusive coverage of the chase, and it was soon joined by nearly a dozen others. Already, the case had become a media circus.

One radio station contacted Simpson's former coach, John McKay, who went live on air to beg Simpson to give himself up. Meanwhile, thousands of curious spectators thronged overpass roads along the route waiting to catch a glimpse of the rolling crime scene. By this time, a staggering 95 million people around the world were watching on TV.

The 50-mile chase ended at 8.00pm outside Simpson's Brentwood home, and Simpson was allowed to go inside before his attorney, Robert Shapiro, arrived and suggested Simpson turn himself in.

There was more drama to come, and it began to unfold rapidly. A grand jury, called to determine whether to indict Simpson for the two murders, was dismissed two days later when it was considered that the media frenzy would prejudice its decision. Then a man who might have been a key witness was dismissed after selling his story to the newspapers. Jose Camacho, a knife salesman at Ross Cutlery, claimed that had he sold Simpson a 15-inch German knife similar to the

Blood Trail at Bundy

ABOVE: Los Angeles Police Detective Tom Lange (left) pointing to pictures of the trail of blood at Nicole Brown Simpson's condominium where she and her friend Ron Goldman were murdered, during testimony in the O. J. Simpson murder trial.

LEFT: O. J. Simpson reacting as a coroner describes the autopsy report on Nicole Brown Simpson in court in 1995.

murder weapon three weeks before the fatal attacks. A female witness who claimed she saw Simpson driving away from Nicole's home on the night of the murders was forbidden to give evidence for the same reason. Nevertheless, after a week-long court hearing, a California Superior Court judge ruled on July 7, that there was ample evidence to try Simpson. At his second court appearance, on July 23, Simpson stated, "Absolutely, one hundred percent, not guilty."

Amid a welter of media attention, the trial began on January 25, 1995. Los Angeles County prosecutor Christopher Darden stated that Simpson had killed his ex-wife in a jealous rage and opened the case by playing an emergency 911 call made by Nicole Brown Simpson on January 1, 1989. The jury heard Nicole crying out that Simpson was going to attack her, while her husband could be heard shouting threateningly at her in the background.

The prosecution continued to produce what seemed like damning evidence: Simpson had a history of violence toward his wife and dozens of expert witnesses testified that DNA, fingerprints, blood, and shoe prints clearly placed Simpson at the scene of the crime. All evidence, it was alleged, pointed to a murder during which Simpson had forced Nicole to the ground, grabbed her hair to pull her head back, put his foot on her back, and slit her throat as she lay face down on the ground. A trail of blood spots had been identified leading from Nicole's house to Simpson's Bronco and his own home on Rockingham Drive.

While this evidence alone looked convincing, even more was produced. Simpson had last been seen in public on the night of the murders at 9.36pm when he returned to his house with Brian "Kato" Kaelin, a bit-part actor, after which they had eaten at a nearby McDonald's. Simpson was not seen again until 10.54pm when he got into a limousine and went to LAX Airport to fly to Chicago. During the time the murders took place no alibi could be given. Simpson had also been spotted driving the Bronco to and from the scene during the time both prosecution and defence agreed the murder had been committed. The driver of the limo the accused would later take to the airport reported that he had arrived at Simpson's home around 10.30pm and rung the doorbell, but got no answer. He then saw Simpson come home about 15 minutes' later. At first Simpson's excuse for not answering the bell was that he had overslept. Another witness, a neighbor, said he heard "three loud thumps" and went out to investigate. The two men both said they had seen Simpson outside, looking agitated. Further evidence showed that DNA samples from

BELOW: Prosecutor Brain Kelberg points to a chart showing where wounds were inflicted on murder victim Ronald Goldman in the O. J. Simpson murder trial.

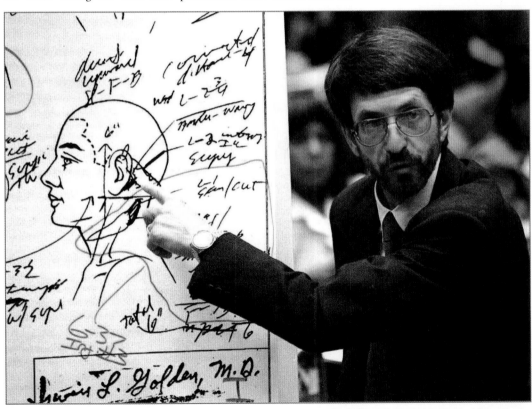

ABOVE: O. J. Simpson showing the jury a new pair of Aris extra-large gloves, similar to those found at the crime scene.

bloody footprints leading away from the bodies and from the back gate of the condominium matched Simpson's blood.

Although no actual murder weapon had been found, and no further witnesses had come forward save those who had earlier been dismissed, the prosecution was confident of a conviction.

Now it was the turn of Simpson's top-flight defence team, which had been described by the press as a "Dream Team." It comprised lawyers F. Lee Bailey, Robert Shapiro, Alan Dershowitz, Robert Kardashian, Gerald Uelmen (a law professor at Santa Clara University), Carl E. Douglas, and Cochran, as well as Peter Neufeld and Barry Scheck, two attorneys specializing in DNA evidence. They swiftly set out to destroy the evidence, alleging that Simpson was the victim of police fraud and that "sloppy internal procedures" had contaminated the DNA evidence.

Further to this, they claimed that Simpson had not left his house that evening, but had been busy packing for his trip to Chicago, save for a short break during which he had gone outside to hit golf balls into a children's sandpit in the front garden—hence the three loud thumps on the wall of the neighbor's bungalow. The Spanish-speaking housekeeper of another neighbor testified that she had seen Simpson's car parked outside his house at the time of the murders. When challenged, however, she said she could not be sure of the exact time she had seen the car. But adding weight to the defence was the evidence of an airport check-in clerk who said Simpson appeared perfectly normal at LAX airport on the night of the murders.

The defence also suggested that Simpson was not physically capable of carrying out the murders; Ronald Goldman was a fit young man who had put up a fierce struggle against his attacker while Simpson had chronic arthritis. To counter this, one of the prosecuting team, Marcia Clark, showed an exercise video that Simpson made two years earlier.

The most famous piece of evidence was till to come though: a glove carrying traces of Goldman's DNA that had been found at Simpson's house. Cochran goaded

BELOW: O. J. Simpson reacting to the not guilty verdict at his criminal trial for the murders of his ex-wife and Ron Goldman.

an assistant prosecutor into asking Simpson to put the glove on. It appeared too tight, prompting Gerald Uelman to tell the jury, "If it doesn't fit, you must acquit." Police had planted the glove in Simpson's house, they claimed. Prosecutor Darden would refute that Simpson was framed in his closing arguments, pointing out that police had visited his house eight times on domestic violence calls without arresting him before eventually citing him for abuse in 1989.

Ripples from the Simpson case were felt far and wide during the trial, and stirred racial tension between black communities in which many thought Simpson a victim of injustice and white communities where a majority believed he was guilty. It also caused a storm of argument over media coverage of trials.

Following a trial of over eight months the not guilty verdict was returned by a majority African American jury at 10.00am on October 3, 1995. After long months

ABOVE: Lou Brown (left) and Juditha Brown (right), the parents of Nicole Brown Simpson, with their attorney John Kelley (centre) outside the Santa Monica, California, courthouse, following the guilty verdicts in the O.J Simpson wrongful death civil trial.

of hearing the evidence they deliberated over the decision for just four hours. In all, 150 witnesses had given testimony and media coverage was unprecedented throughout. Simpson's defence was said to have cost between three and six million dollars.

Nevertheless, there were still more dramas and revelations to come. In post-trial interviews a few jurors said that they believed Simpson probably committed the murders, but that the prosecution had bungled the case. Three of them later published a book called Madam Foreman, in which they described how police errors, not race, led to their verdict, and that they considered prosecutor Darden to be a "token black" assigned to the case. A year later, both the Brown and Goldman families sued Simpson for damages in a civil trial. On February 5, 1997, the jury unanimously found there was sufficient evidence to find Simpson liable for damages in the wrongful death of Goldman and battery of Brown. In its conclusions, the jury effectively found Simpson liable for the death of his ex-wife and Ron Goldman, although the burden of proof is lower in civil cases than in criminal ones. Yet another indication that Simpson's acquittal may have been a miscarriage of justice came in September 2004, when porn star Jennifer Peace came forward claiming that she was Al Cowlings' girlfriend and that Cowlings—who had been in the car with Simpson during the famous chase—had told her that Simpson confessed his guilt. In 2008, Mike Gilbert released his book *How I Helped O. J. Get Away with Murder*, which told how Simpson had also confessed to him.

Yvonne Sleightholme

At first glance the killing of Jayne Smith by a former girlfriend of her husband appears to be a straightforward case of a murder committed by an unbalanced woman in a frenzy of jealousy. However, Yvonne Sleightholme has always maintained her innocence and after she was convicted evidence came to light that suggests there may be a shred of truth to her claims. Nevertheless, she served six years more in prison than the judge at her trial recommended.

Yvonne Sleightholme, a doctor's receptionist, met William Smith at a disco nightclub in Yorkshire 1979, and the two began a relationship soon after. But while they talked of weddings Smith began to have doubts about his girlfriend and, growing weary of her controlling nature, he eventually finished with her. Yvonne took it badly and lied that she was dying of leukemia. Out of sympathy Smith briefly took her back, but it soon became obvious that there was nothing physically wrong with Yvonne and meanwhile he had met Jayne, who he would later marry. The relationship with Yvonne ended once again.

On December 12, 1989, the body of Jayne Smith was found in the yard of the couple's farm at Salton in the Yorkshire Dales, England. It looked like an attempted rape gone wrong; her clothes were in disarray and her body scratched. She had died of a gunshot wound fired at point blank range into the back of her head. There was a strange irregularity about the killing though, and one that would lead straight back to Yvonne Sleightholme. Jayne's attacker had taken the trouble to remove her wedding ring. It spoke of a murder committed out of jealousy rather than lust.

At her trial in May 1991, Yvonne claimed she had been at the farm on the night of the murder, but had had nothing to do with it. Mr Justice Waite, prosecuting, argued that after her fiancé had broken off their engagement and later married another woman, the already unstable Sleightholme had been twisted by envy and "wrought upon the newly-married couple a terrible revenge." The jury was convinced. Yvonne was found guilty of murder and sentenced to life in prison, with a recommendation that she should serve at least ten years.

Several years later, Yvonne's supporters came up with new evidence that seemed to cast doubt on the court's decision. A bloody handprint had been found in her car, but it was too large to have been made by her. Nevertheless, Yvonne's hopes of taking her case back to the Court of Appeal were dashed when judges threw out the application. Still she protested that she was innocent and, in January 2002, gave an interview to the local evening paper from Styal Prison in Cheshire. She told the reporter that she would never admit to killing Jayne Smith, saying, "I value the truth more than anything… I didn't do it, and nothing—not even the chance of freedom—will make me lie and say I did it. I was not responsible for that terrible murder."

In March 2003, the Yorkshire Evening Post newspaper revealed it had obtained documents proving Sleightholme had been an exemplary prisoner, and that she was not, as had been claimed, likely to commit another violent act. The editor wrote to the parole board, asking for it to look again at the application, and Ryedale member of Parliament John Greenway passed the documents on to a government minister. The following month, the then Home Secretary David Blunkett referred the case back to the board for a fresh review. Following this, Sleightholme was transferred to an open prison, Askham Grange near York, finally being released in December 2005 after 16 years in prison.

BELOW: Yvonne Sleightholme being helped into Leeds Crown Court, to face charges for the murder of Jayne Smith.

Pam Smart and Billy Flynn

Pam Smart began a fling with one of the boys at the school where she worked in order to get back at her cheating husband and never expected to fall in love with a 16-year-old boy. When she did, she conspired with her lover to remove the man who stood in the way of their future together. She should have remembered that it is impossible to keep secrets in the classroom.

The marriage of Pam Smart and her insurance salesman husband Greg was already rocky by the time that he came back from a business trip and confessed that he had had a one-night stand while he was away. Pam was furious and determined to level the score with him. She was 21 and attractive, and had always had a certain sexual allure. It was obvious that William Flynn, one of the boys at the school where she worked, had long had a crush on her, so Pam set out to teach the young student a few things he would never have learned in the classroom while taking revenge on her cheating husband.

Pam and Flynn were soon having sex whenever they could and at some point Pam realized that what had started out as a casual thing had become much, much more. Now she constantly craved the attentions of her teenage lover and was deeply infatuated with him. She wanted Flynn so much more than she wanted Greg Smart, but instead of a lengthy divorce, her thoughts turned to getting Smart out of the way a little more speedily.

She confided in Flynn and at first the boy was shocked by her plan, but his older lover was persuasive and soon he had agreed to what looked like a foolproof murder plot. He recruited two of his best friends, Pete Randall and Vance Lattime, to help and another, Raymond Fowler, would go along with them just for the ride. On May 1, 1990, having been married for less than a year, Pam was at a school meeting, which gave her a perfect alibi. Greg Smart was at their home Derry, New

LEFT: Pamela Smart on the witness stand during her trial at Rockingham County Superior Court in Exeter, New Hampshire.

three boys involved in the killing by their first names. Flynn, Randall, and Lattime were arrested on June 11, 1990. Flynn was charged with first degree murder, the other two with being accomplices to first degree murder. Pam Smart was arrested at work on August 1, 1990 with the officer, Dan Pelletier telling her, "Well Pam, I've got good news and I've got bad news. The good news is we've solved the murder of your husband. The bad news is you're under arrest."

The trial of Pam Smart and the three boys began on March 5, 1991. With its ingredients of a young attractive woman involved with the murder of her husband after seducing a teenage student, it attracted

ABOVE: Vance Lattime giving evidence against Pam Smart in Rockingham County Superior Court in Exeter, New Hampshire.

BELOW: William Flynn appearing at Rockingham Superior Court in Brentwood, New Hampshire in 2008. Flynn, was seeking a sentence reduction.

Hampshire, when the boys entered the house, shot him in the head, and quickly made the scene look like a badly botched burglary. On returning home, Pam discovered the body and—pretending to be devastated—called in the police.

But teenage boys are never very discreet. Randall and Lattime were overheard talking about the killing and another pupil, Cecelia Pierce went to the police. She agreed to co-operate with them and made recorded phone calls in which she encouraged Pam to give details of the murder plot.

Hers was not the only accusation the police heard. Flynn told a friend that he shot Greg Smart because he beat his wife and gossip and rumor spread like wildfire in the schoolyard. The police department received an anonymous phone call informing them that "the school teacher was sleeping with one of the boys and she staged the whole thing." The caller mentioned all huge media attention. The jury went out on May 20 and deliberated for 13 hours before finding Pam guilty on three counts; conspiracy to commit murder, accomplice to a murder, and tampering with a witness. She was sentenced to life imprisonment. Flynn and Randall each received 40 years with a parole review in 2018. Lattime was sentenced to 30 years, but released in 2006. Fowler also received a prison sentence, later extended because of a parole violation. He was eventually released in 2005.

Madeleine Smith

The 19th century is notorious for its strictly enforced morality, particularly when it concerned the behavior of wealthy young women. The slightest sin could permanently ruin a girl's reputation, bring shame on the family, and wreck her hopes of a good marriage. And for a girl to lose her virginity out of wedlock was the ultimate crime, so for 19-year-old Madeleine Smith the threat of a previous sexual dalliance being revealed to her family and new fiancé was a peril worth killing to prevent.

Madeleine was the daughter of a prosperous Scottish architect and enjoyed all the trappings of her father's wealth; a busy social life in her native Glasgow as well as a large country home. Unfortunately, her carefree lifestyle would come to an abrupt end. It began when friends introduced her to a dashing young Frenchman in the street. Pierre Emile L'Angelier was an apprentice nurseryman staying in Glasgow and immediately caught Madeleine's eye. The young girl was overwhelmed by her new passion and began to meet L'Angelier in secret whenever it could be arranged, and when a meeting was impossible she poured out her feelings in letters, addressing them to "my own darling husband."

Their love was chaste for months, and could later have been explained away as a girlish crush had this continued. But that was to change during an unchaperoned visit to the family house in the country that Madeleine managed to arrange. In secret, L'Angelier followed his wealthy young love, and with her parents absent their desire for each other could be contained no longer. Afterward, she wrote another of her gushing letters to L'Angelier, telling him, "If we did wrong last night it was in the excitement of our love." The couple became unofficially engaged.

In those days when a young woman's conduct was watched carefully, it was inevitable that Madeleine would eventually be found out. Sure enough, her parents soon became aware of their daughter's illicit affair with a mere apprentice. Although Madeleine managed to keep from them the information about the loss of her virginity, they were shocked and instantly ordered an end to the affair. And it seems that Madeleine had become bored of her lover anyway, and certainly didn't waste any time pining for him. Soon after, she was introduced to a wealthy bachelor named William Harper Minnoch. There was an instant attraction between the two of them, and this time Madeleine was given her parents' blessing for what, after all, was a much better match. The only fly in Madeleine's ointment was her former beau.

L'Angelier had kept all of Madeleine's letters, which contained unmistakable references to the fact that she had surrendered her virginity to him. Knowing how devastating these would be if they ever became public knowledge, she wrote to him, begging that the letters be returned so that she could destroy them. The spurned L'Angelier had other ideas however. Instead, he threatened to reveal all to Madeleine's father unless she honored her promise to marry him.

Her response was to hatch a plot that would forever silence the man who had the power to ruin her reputation and with it her future happiness. Not long after, a woman was seen in a shop buying arsenic. She signed for the poison in the name of M. H. Smith. Meanwhile, Madeleine had continued writing to L'Angelier and lulled him with sweet words and protestations of undying love. Soon, she had managed to arrange another meeting, smuggling the young man into the basement of the family's Glasgow home. During the visit she kept up the appearance of a young girl still in love, while serving her blackmailer cocoa laced with arsenic.

Madeleine played her part so well that L'Angelier suspected nothing when he became ill soon after their meeting. As soon as he was able, he returned to Madeleine's basement. And a second cup of cocoa. This one would prove fatal. Within hours, L'Angelier fell gravely ill and in less than a day, he was dead. His doctor, mystified at L'Angelier's symptoms, ordered a postmortem that revealed 87 grains of arsenic still in his patient's stomach. It did not take the police long to discover a bundle of Madeleine's letters at L'Angelier's lodgings, and the tale they told gave investigating officers a prime suspect for the murder. Madeleine was arrested on March 31, 1857. She stood trial soon after.

Her defense told the jury that Madeleine had bought arsenic to use as rat poison and maintained that L'Angelier had often taken arsenic himself for health reasons. It was a flimsy argument and all evidence pointed to her having murdered her former lover. Nevertheless, it was deemed circumstantial, and not enough to convict her. Instead, a verdict of "not proven" was given, which in Scottish courts means that the jury does not believe the accused to be innocent, though the prosecution has failed to make a strong enough case. Fortunately for Madeleine

what would have been a key witness—a person who had seen her together with a male companion on the night of the poisoning—was not allowed to testify. They had come forward too late and the trial had already started. Madeleine walked free from the court, but was widely believed to be guilty of murder. Her engagement to William Minnoch came to an abrupt end, and instead she married George Wardle before leaving Scotland—and the scandal—behind for good.

BELOW: A contemporary illustration of Madeleine Smith, from around the time of her trial for the murder of her former lover Pierre Emile L'Anglier.

Susan Smith

However grisly and twisted the murder, most of us can understand how a thwarted love or systematic abuse might lead someone to a killing rage. Susan Smith's crime though, went far beyond that. It is one thing to murder a cheating lover, but to take the lives of your own children is on a level of horror all its own.

The crime of three-year-old Michael and his 14-month-old brother Alex was that they came between their mother and the man she wanted to be with. Recently divorced, struggling to cope, and becoming deeper in debt with every month that passed, 23-year-old Susan Smith was desperate for the security that her relationship with Tom Findlay might bring. He, however, was not ready to step into a ready-made family and wrote to tell her that though he cared deeply for her, he was just not ready for the responsibility. As he would later strenuously point out, at no point did he make any suggestion that Susan should somehow get rid of her children.

Nevertheless, that is exactly what Susan decided she needed to do. Although she might have given them over to the custody of their father, instead she strapped them into the back of her car, took the emergency

BELOW: Police mug shots of Susan Smith released by the South Carolina Department of Corrections after her arrest in 1994.

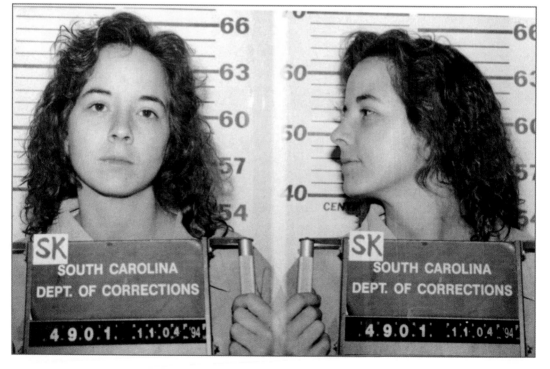

ABOVE: A shrine at John D. Long Lake, South Carolina, featuring toys and pictures of Michael and Alex Smith, who were murdered by their mother Susan.

brake off, and let it roll downhill and into a lake where the two boys drowned.

At about 9.15pm on October 25, 1994, the police took a call from a hysterical woman. Smith told them that she had been driving her two children home in Union, South Carolina, when a young black man had forced his way into the car while she was stopped at a red light. At gunpoint, he demanded Smith drive off and then pushed her out of the car a few miles down the road, before driving away with her two boys still strapped into the back seat.

A huge manhunt immediately swept into operation and the eyes of America fastened on the devastated young woman. But the television appeals of Smith and her estranged husband David produced no results, and the search, too, was a failure. Puzzled by the lack of success, nine days after the boys had gone missing the police again questioned Smith to see if there might be some detail not yet mentioned which might help them. This time she broke down and confessed to her terrible crime. Police divers were sent to search the lake and quickly found her Mazda not far beneath the surface, with her sons dead in the back. Smith was charged with first degree murder.

The trial of Susan Smith began amid a whirl of media attention on July 18, 1995. It was to become one of the most avidly followed and harrowing court cases the United States has ever witnessed. From the start the prosecution were determined that the jury understood the severity of the crime, and the details heard in court were shocking. One diver recalled the moment that he had shone his flashlight at the car and through the murky water had seen "a small hand against the glass." Lawyers defending Smith argued that it was not murder, but a suicide attempt gone awry. Rejected by the man she had hoped might turn her life around, they told the jury that Smith had wanted to take her own life along with her sons'. They also painted a detailed picture of Susan's life up to that point—the alcoholic father who had committed suicide, the sexual abuse she had suffered as a child, and the desolation she carried with her every day.

It was a powerful defense and in her closing speech, Judge Judy Clarke asked the jury to show mercy toward Smith, telling them that she had made the decision "with a confused mind and a heart that has no hope." Nevertheless, the sheer horror of Smith's crime was more powerful. On July 28, 1995, she was found guilty of the murder of her two sons. Her sentence was life, with no possibility of parole until 2025.

Paul Snider

To marry a woman who turns heads whenever she walks into a room can be difficult for an insecure man. For Paul Snider, whose wife was Playmate of the Year in *Playboy* magazine, the attention she received was more than enough to turn him mad with jealousy, and when she divorced him and became involved with one of Hollywood's great directors, his envy became a killing rage.

Dorothy Stratten was plain Dorothy Hoogstratten when Paul Snider walked into the Dairy Queen in Vancouver, Canada, where she worked in 1977. She was stunningly beautiful and he was a man on the up. After seducing her, Snider began taking sexy photos of his lover and eventually managed to get them published in the men's magazine *Playboy*. Dorothy's sex appeal did not go unnoticed, and soon the couple were invited to join in the fun at *Playboy* founder Hugh Hefner's "Playboy Mansion." At first Snider was happy for Dorothy to indulge in sexual frolics with the other guests; it was good for her career—and for his bank balance. But Snider hadn't stopped to consider how attached he had become to Dorothy. As he realized that he had fallen in love with her so his jealousy grew.

The couple married in Las Vegas in June 1979. In August, Dorothy was Playmate of the Month. Dorothy was 20 and Snider, 29. At the time, Snider's new wife told friends that she couldn't imagine being with anyone but Paul. However, Snider was now obsessed with Dorothy's career and was increasingly controlling. He forbade her to drink coffee, because it would stain her teeth, and it is rumored that he also poisoned her pet dog because he was jealous of it. Dorothy couldn't ignore his erratic behavior for long, and the marriage crumbled. After a year if marriage they filed for divorce. Life in 1980 was good for Dorothy—she was Playmate of the Year. Free of the man who thought he had discovered her, she began seeing film director Peter Bogdanovich then moved into his Bel Air home.

Snider had lost both the woman he loved and the key to success and riches. He took a distinctly sinister turn. He hired a private investigator to follow Dorothy.

On the morning of August 14, 1980, Dorothy agreed to meet Snider at the apartment they once shared. She arrived with a large handbag containing $1,000 to pay off her ex-husband. It was around 11pm that the private investigator finally got an answer from the numerous phone calls he made to the apartment. He told one of the women who lodged with Snider that he had been trying the number all day and asked her to check on her landlord. When she did, she found Dorothy lying across Snider's waterbed, dead from a bullet would. She was missing the tip of her left index finger, blown off as she tried to protect her face.

Close by was the body of Snider. He had shot himself. Examination of the scene revealed that Dorothy had been sexually brutalized both before and after she died. She was cremated and buried on August 19, at Westwood Memorial Park.

BELOW: Playboy Playmate Dorothy Stratten in May 1980.

Dr. James Howard Snook

For three years the wealthy and successful Dr. James Snook met his young lover several times a week in the rooms he rented so that they might have a comfortable place to have sex. But somewhere their relationship went awry. What started out as a purely physical affair ended with Theora Hix laying dead in a patch of weeds, battered with a hammer and her throat slit.

Doctor Snook was successful and confident man to whom life had been kind. He was a professor of Veterinary Medicine at the Ohio State University in Columbus and a respected horse surgeon. He had also won two Olympic gold medals for pistol shooting and enjoyed the love of his devoted wife Helen and their baby daughter. And in June 1926, soon after giving 21-year-old medical student Theora Hix a lift to the university, he also had a fresh and attractive young sexual partner. After spending a day at work, Snook visited Theora in the rooms he rented. The couple would make love in the early evenings then the doctor would return home to his wife. As Snook would

later testify, neither he nor Theora were in love, the relationship was purely sexual. For a relationship that was all about sex though, something was amiss. Theora taunted her older lover about his sexual performance and even went so far as to recommend books he might read to improve his technique.

Nevertheless, the relationship continued. On one occasion, after a break-in at her university room, Snook gave Theora a Remington Derringer pistol for protection, and the two began going to the New York Central Rifle Range on the outskirts of Columbus to practise. It was here that two 16-year-old boys discovered her body on June 16, 1929. She had been beaten around the head and her throat was cut. The body was soon identified; Theora's roommates had already reported her missing and when her photograph appeared in the local newspaper, Mrs Margaret Smalley recognized Theora as the young "wife" of a man called Howard Snook who rented the room from her.

When Snook was arrested, police found blood inside his car, on the clothing he wore the night of the murder, on his ball-peen hammer, and on his pocket knife. He had tried to clean everything, but enough traces remained to declare his guilt.

Exactly why Snook's passions were roused to the point where a previously law-abiding man would beat a young woman to death will never be known. The only testimony we have is Snook's, and he had good reason to construct a story that would help the jury see him as a victim of a jealous lover's threats. In fact at his trial, Snook testified that he and Theora had driven to a local country club to make love. Once they arrived, she had told him that she wanted to go "some place where I can scream," and Snook had taken her on to the New York Central shooting range.

Snook then told Theora that he then had to go as he was due to visit his mother. At this point, he said, Theora became angry shouting, "Damn your mother. I don't care about your mother. Damn Mrs Snook. I'm going to kill her and get her out of the way." Snook said she then continued to threaten his family, even saying she would kill his daughter. He went on to testify that she had grabbed open his trousers and began to bite and pull at him. In fear for his safety and for his family's lives, Snook said he grabbed the ball-peen hammer from his kit in the back of the car and hit her with it. Theora then screamed, "Damn you, I will kill you too." According to Snook, she began digging through her purse. Afraid that she was looking for the Derringer pistol, he hit her on the head with the hammer several times until she fell to the ground.

We should approach this tale with caution, for Snook's explanation of Theora's cut throat changed over time. At first he said he did not know how her neck had come to be cut open, but it was pointed out to him that it had been cut so precisely that only someone experienced in anatomy and surgery—such as a veterinarian—could have done it. He then said that he had cut her throat because he did not want to see her suffer from the head wounds.

On August 14, 1929, Snook was found guilty of first degree murder and sentenced to death in the Ohio Penitentiary's electric chair. Before the day of his execution arrived, his story changed again. Snook supposedly confessed to a warden that the murder had been premeditated. After several attempts to obtain a new trial or change the verdict to manslaughter or second degree murder, Snook was executed on February 28, 1930.

Ruth Snyder

Ruth Snyder led a double life: To her husband she was a doting wife and mother, and to her lover she was a domineering sexual mistress. But dissatisfaction, coupled with a good helping of greed, would lead her and her lover to try and make her double life a single life.

At the age of 20, in 1895, Ruth Sorensen was an attractive and charming young operator at a New York City telephone exchange where one bungled call changed her life and set in motion a train of events that would eventually lead to murder. The call was between a man named Albert Schneider, who was the art editor of a magazine called *Motor Boat*, and his client. Ruth was so sincere and appealing in her apology for having messed it up that Schneider offered her a job as a

RIGHT: A photograph of Ruth Snyder taken in 1927, the year that she murdered her husband.

secretary on the magazine. Before a year had passed they were married, and afterward changed their names to Snyder to avert some of the anti-German feeling that was then common.

Seemingly a perfect suburban couple, their home on Long Island soon welcomed the arrival of a baby, and Ruth sank all her energies into being as good a mother and wife she could be. And for a while she enjoyed it. Her husband, however, was not so happy. He was domineering, prone to outbursts of temper, and found domestic life boring. The two began to lead separate lives, neither questioning the other about where they were or with whom.

Young, attractive, and all but deserted by her husband, Ruth invited her mother to move into the house, and with a permanent babysitter on call, began a series of affairs, the most serious of which was with corset salesman Henry Judd Gray. Theirs was an unusual sexual relationship, with Ruth now taking on the dominant role and Gray enjoying subservience. The two would later be labelled by the press "Granite Woman and Putty Man."

The only thing that stood in the way of Ruth's total freedom was her husband and the money he brought in to support her and the baby. However, Ruth soon came up with a plan to solve both problems.

Back in her role as the concerned wife, Ruth persuaded her husband to purchase a life insurance policy and with the assistance of an agent (who was subsequently imprisoned for forgery) she signed an additional $48,000 policy that paid extra if an unexpected act of violence killed the victim. She then made a series of botched attempts to kill Snyder, all of which he survived.

But on March 20, 1927, with the help of Gray, Ruth finally succeeded. When Snyder was safely asleep in bed, the couple sneaked into his room, smashed his head, garroted him, and stuffed his nose full of chloroform–soaked rags. They then made a hasty attempt to make it look like the Snyders had been victims of a burglary gone wrong. Ruth got Gray to tie up her ankles and wrists, but managed to "break free" to raise the alarm while her lover fled the scene.

It didn't take detectives long to unpick the lies. Ruth was betrayed by many small clues. The police wondered why when she had undone her wrists she had not untied her ankles as well. And whoever had attacked Albert had gone out of their way to kill him, which didn't fit into the pattern of a burglary. Finally, property that Ruth said had been stolen started turning up in odd places around the house. Then detectives came across a letter signed "J.G." Snyder tried to convince them the initials were those of a young woman that her husband had once dated, but a flip through Ruth's address book revealed the names of a total of 28 men. One was Judd Gray.

Eventually though it was Ruth who declared her guilt. When the police took her in for questioning and told her that they already had Gray in custody and that he had confessed everything. She crumbled and the whole story spilled out. In fact, it was a standard police trick. At that time they hadn't even caught up with Gray though he was arrested at a hotel in Syracuse later that night.

Both Judd Gray and Ruth Snyder were charged with murder, and the case went to trial on April 18, 1927. Each tried to blame the other for the murder, but the jury found both guilty and they were sentenced to death. They were executed on January 12, 1928. Ruth Snyder would later achieve a degree of grim fame after a reporter took a picture of her dying in the electric chair with a miniature camera strapped to his ankle.

George Stoner

A difference in age is no barrier to love, as Alma Rattenbury found out when she advertised for a boy to help around the home she shared with her husband. She would also find out that the young are just as prone as their elders to jealousy.

No stranger to scandal, 39-year-old Alma Rattenbury and her 67-year-old husband Francis had been forced to flee their home in Canada by wagging tongues. He had been married when he began his affair with Alma and, soon after, asked his wife for a divorce. When she refused, he simply moved his mistress into the family home until eventually his wife agreed to part. Inevitably, the details of this scheme to force an innocent woman into divorce became public knowledge and the criticism of Alma and Rattenbury was so great that they crossed the Atlantic to seek a quiet life in Bournemouth, England.

Unfortunately, a quiet life was not what they found. The couple bought a large house and moved in with Alma's thirteen-year-old son Christopher from an earlier marriage, and the couple's six-year-old son John.

They soon found that a little extra help would be needed to run the house, and Alma placed a notice in the Bournemouth Echo advertising a position for a, "Daily willing lad, 14–18, for house-work; scout-trained preferred. Apply between 11–12, 8–9 at 5 Manor Road, Bournemouth."

The willing lad who answered was the handsome but shy George Stoner. In fact, Alma found him very willing indeed: as well as his household chores, Stoner soon found very pleasant extra duties in Alma's bed. He quickly became so indispensable that his part-time position was changed to full time and he was given a

BELOW: A long queue of people forming outside the Old Bailey court for the trial of Alma Rattenbury and George Stoner, jointly charged with the murder of Francis Rattenbury.

ABOVE: Petitioners trying to persuade railway staff at Waterloo Station, London to add their names to the petition appealing to the Home Secretary to grant a reprieve George Stoner.

room in the house. Francis Rattenbury was fully aware of his wife's infidelity, but now slipping into old age he had become impotent and turned a blind eye, much preferring to share his evenings with a bottle of whiskey and let his wife have her fun.

For a while the unorthodox situation appeared to work well, but as time progressed Stoner fell ever more deeply in love with his sophisticated older mistress, and grew jealous of her elderly husband. Greedy for every moment with her, he became upset when she spent time with Rattenbury and flew into a rage when the husband and wife went away for a weekend together. Convinced that Rattenbury was finally trying to win his wife back, when they returned and Alma told him that they would also be away the following weekend, Stoner's jealousy finally got the better of him.

On the afternoon of March 24, 1935, Stoner borrowed a wooden mallet from his grandparents, telling them that he needed it to erect a screen in the garden. Later that evening, Francis Rattenbury was found seriously injured. He had been bludgeoned on the head from behind. Three days later he died from his injuries and what had previously been an assault case became a murder.

The police immediately questioned Alma, who appeared to be the worse for wear through drink or drugs. Perhaps she originally intended to take the blame, for over and over she kept repeating that she had "done him in." Nevertheless, soon after, Stoner confessed to another servant, Irene Riggs, that it was he who had dealt the killer blow that did for Rattenbury. She went to the police. Alma and Stoner were both arrested and charged with murder.

The lovers were tried together at the Old Bailey on May 27, 1935. Both pleaded not guilty with a now sober Alma passionately claiming she had nothing to do with her husband's death. Stoner was quiet in court, but his defense counsel suggested that though he had hit Rattenbury in a jealous rage, he had not intended to kill. The jury did not agree. Stoner was found guilty and sentenced to death. Alma was acquitted much to the consternation of the crowd waiting outside. In their eyes, a three-times married older woman had led an innocent young lad to kill.

A few days later, Alma took the train from Waterloo to Christchurch, not far from her Bournemouth home. She sat down on the banks of a river and wrote a handful of farewell notes. Then she plunged a knife several times into her heart, and died almost immediately. It is clear from the notes and from the words of a song she wrote while awaiting trial—subsequently published as *Mrs Rattenbury's Prison Song*—that she was deeply in love with Stoner, and took her own life out of grief for her loss and shame at what had happened. Stoner, when informed of her death, broke down and wept.

Alma was buried a few yards from her late husband, and during the ceremony signatures were collected for an appeal for mercy for George Stoner. Over the next few weeks an astonishing 320,000 people, including the local mayor and MP, signed the petition. It was handed to the Home Secretary, who commuted Stoner's sentence to penal servitude for life. A model prisoner, he was released seven years later in 1942. He died in Christchurch Hospital in 2000 aged 83 on the 65th anniversary of Francis's murder.

John Sweeney

Sweeney's crime of passion was a straightforward fit of selfish anger directed at a talented young actress who he had tried to love him despite the fact that he beat her. When she finished the relationship and refused to take him back, his rage was fatal.

Dominique Dunne was just 21 and a promising actress with a bright future when she met 25-year-old chef John Sweeney at a Hollywood party in 1981. She had been born locally, in Santa Monica, California, but after her parents divorced had moved to New York City, before returning to Los Angeles to try for a Hollywood acting career. Within two weeks she had won her first job and the following year would land her first major movie role as Dana Freeling in the 1982 horror classic *Poltergeist*.

But while Dominique's career was doing well, her relationship was causing problems. Sweeney was the eldest son of a troubled family and had emotional difficulties. At first these manifested themselves in jealousy and attempts to control Dominique. He was suspicious of everyone she met, dominating, and would often show up at film sets, rehearsals, and Dominique's acting classes to watch over her.

However, on August 27, 1982, the couple had their first major quarrel, and Dominique got her first taste of the violence that the man she loved was capable of. Sweeney grabbed her by her hair and slammed her head on the floor so roughly that he pulled out handfuls of her hair.

A month later they had another argument and this time Sweeney threw Dominique to the floor and began to choke her. Luckily a friend was present and intervened. The next day Dominique went to work on an episode of *Hill Street Blues*. Ironically her part was that of an abuse victim. Not all of her bruises were applied by the make-up artist's brush.

By now, the actress had had enough. She finished the relationship with Sweeney and changed the locks on

BELOW: Restaurant chef John Sweeney sitting in a courtroom in Beverly Hills, California, during his trial for the murder of actress Dominique Dunne.

the doors of the house they once shared. Sweeney wasn't prepared to let his girlfriend go without a fight though. On October 30, 1982, Dominique was at the house rehearsing a scene for a television series with a fellow actor, David Parker, when her ex-boyfriend arrived. There was a fierce argument that ended with Sweeney strangling the young star, putting her in a coma. She died in hospital on November 4, aged just 22. Dominique had been working on a new TV series when she was attacked. On the credits of the second episode were the words "In loving memory of Dominique Dunne, her family and friends miss her."

John Thomas Sweeney was charged with murder and the case came to trial in August 1983 in Santa Monica. Incredibly, Sweeney's lawyer, Michael Adelson, argued that Dominique was to blame for her own death, saying that she had provoked the violent struggle because she refused to be reconciled with Sweeney. On the witness stand Sweeney himself said he "just exploded and lunged toward her" and added that he said he had no memory of what happened next. Adelson argued it was not a real crime, but an act of despair.

The police evidence, however, told a different story. According to the officers who arrested him Sweeney seemed to be quite calm and collected—and much more interested in his own fate than in Dominique's—when they arrived at the scene. They told how, during his first interrogation, Sweeney had showed no remorse for what he had done. Medical evidence also confirmed that the duration of the strangulation was at least three minutes. If it had been an explosion of anger, there was enough time for

RIGHT: John Sweeney being escorted from the courthouse during his murder trial.

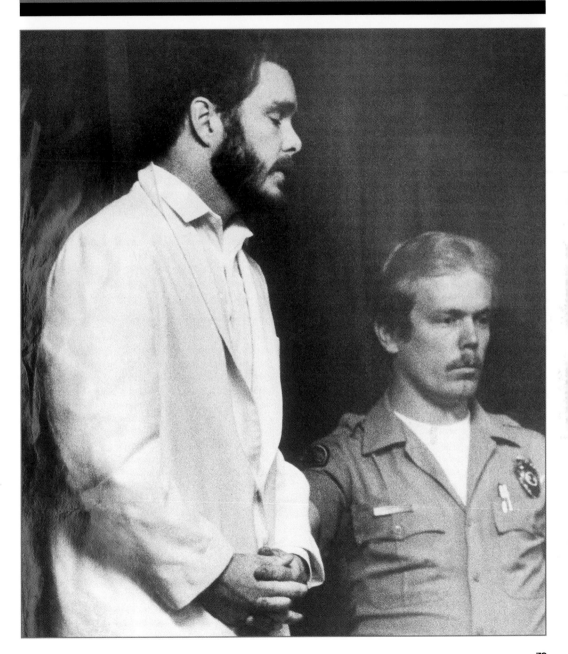

Sweeney to take control of himself. If he had stopped a few seconds earlier it may have saved Dominique's life.

Sweeney was convicted of the voluntary manslaughter of Dominique Dunne and only served two and a half years of a six and a half year prison sentence. Members of the jury later said they would have convicted Sweeney of murder had they been aware of his earlier history of violence against women.

Although the time he served did not seem to reflect the magnitude of his horrific crime, on his release Dominique's mother did not let him slip quietly back into Hollywood life. When Sweeney got another job as chef at a Los Angeles restaurant, Ellen Griffin founded a grievance support group called "Justice for Victims of Homicide." On the nights that John Sweeney worked, she and other group members would hand out slips of paper to the restaurant's customers that read, "The hands that will prepare your meal tonight also murdered Dominique Dunne." John Sweeney soon lost his job and was forced to move to the Pacific Northwest where he changed his name to John Maura.

John Tanner

The disappearance of Rachel McLean hit the headlines of the British press early in 1991, and for over a fortnight her killer fooled both the public and the police. Clever and calm, John Tanner hid his crime well and went on to make appeals for information about her whereabouts.

Bright and young, with a promising future ahead of her, Rachel McLean was studying English Literature at St. Hilda's in Oxford and was just 19 years old when her 22-year-old boyfriend, John Tanner, strangled her to death. He was a British-born New Zealander, studying in Nottingham. As their relationship was deteriorating Rachel complained that Tanner was controlling and possessive. She no longer wanted to see him and started dating other students. Nevertheless, when he said that he wished to visit her, she agreed.

On the evening of April 13, 1991, Rachel waited at Oxford station for Tanner to arrive and when his train was delayed she returned to her home. He followed on by taxi, arriving at around 7.30pm. Various people later reported seeing them together around Oxford the next day, but that would be the last time that Rachel was seen alive. That night, in a fit of jealous rage, Tanner killed his ex-girlfriend.

It took him several hours to find a suitable hiding spot for her body, but when he did it was a good one. There was a closet beneath the stairs and at the back, behind piles of household junk, Tanner discovered an eight inch gap that led to a space beneath the floorboards. He dragged his girlfriend's body into it and then crawled beneath the hallway pulling Rachel to a spot under her own bedroom. Then he covered the body with old carpet and made everything look just as he found it. Tanner then left the house and made his way back to Nottingham, pausing to pen Rachel a brief love letter in which he mentioned how lucky she was that the long-haired man they had met at Oxford station had offered her a lift home.

By April 19, Rachel's friends had begun to realize that something was amiss. She had been due at a meeting with her tutor and to sit an exam in the afternoon, but had missed both. One called her parents to find out if she was okay and was told that they hadn't seen her either and that she had been in Oxford the previous weekend. By April 22, Rachel's disappearance was headline news and a massive search for her was underway. Naturally, her boyfriend wanted to help all he could and spoke movingly of how he had kissed her goodbye at the station a few days earlier. He also mentioned the fictitious long-haired man again, saying that he had joined them for coffee, and that Rachel had seemed to know him.

Police searched Rachel's house and nearby scrubland, while divers dragged the River Cherwell and Rachel's parents made a nationwide appeal at a press conference on April 24th. Still there was no sign on her. A day later a photo-fit image of the man Tanner claimed to have met at the station was released, and by April 28th police had widened the search to include the sewers around her home.

On the 29th, Tanner agreed to appear in a television reconstruction and with a female police officer playing the part of Rachel, he was filmed at Oxford station, reliving the final coffee with his girlfriend and their final kiss. As the last person to see her alive, he was already under suspicion, but said, "I did not kill her. I don't know what happened to her. In my heart of hearts I know she is still alive."

However, by agreeing to take part in the reconstruction he helped seal his own fate. Two people came forward after seeing it. Both remembered Tanner at the station, but neither saw Rachel or a long-haired man. It became even more obvious that Tanner's tale was a lie when police finally discovered her body in the cavity beneath her floorboards. He was immediately arrested at a Nottingham pub, and taken into custody where he refused to answer police questions.

The evidence against him was continuing to mount up though, and Tanner finally broke down and confessed. On May 4, 1991, he was formally charged with the murder of Rachel McLean before magistrates. He was tried for his crime in early December, convicted, and sentenced to life imprisonment. Released 12 years later in 2003, John Tanner

ABOVE: John Tanner, shown during a press conference making an appeal for information about the whereabouts of Rachel McLean.

immediately returned to his home town of Wanganui, New Zealand.

Marie Tarnowska

The crime of Russian Countess Marie Tarnowska was to treat the men who adored her as puppets in her deadly games of intrigue and betrayal. Her cold appetites knew no limits and those who loved her were either ruined or died. Not by her hand, but always she was behind the scenes, pulling the strings.

Born in 1879, Marie was descended from one of the aristocratic houses of Ireland and the daughter of a man who had been made Count Nicholas O'Rke by the Tsar when he emigrated to Russia. At 17 years old, and outstandingly beautiful, she married the wealthy Count Tarnowska. Together they ruled over the glittering aristocratic society of Kiev and their union was blessed with three children. But as time passed, Marie grew bored of married life and developed a taste for exercising the power she had as a countess and as a woman of boundless sexual allure.

One of her early lovers, Alexis Borzlevski, invited her to shoot him through the hand to demonstrate his devotion to her. The incident didn't go unnoticed, and the count then challenged Borzlevski to a duel. Marie's lover was shot dead. Another of her bedmates, Vladimir Stahl, killed himself rather than confront the count at a dueling ground. Yet another was shot dead by the count at a dinner party when Marie deliberately kissed him to provoke her husband. The powerful count was acquitted of the murder on the grounds of his wife's provocation.

Not surprisingly, perhaps, after this spate of incidents the marriage ended, but not before Marie had woven her lethal spell over the lawyer dealing with her divorce. After she toyed with his emotions, Maximillian Prilukoff was prepared to give up his wife and family, career, and fortune to have her. He botched a suicide attempt when she rejected him and the proceeded to follow her around wherever she went, a 19th-century stalker.

Free of her husband's jealousy, Marie traveled to Venice, Italy, and her army of lovers increased. One was young and handsome Nicolas Naumoff, who deserted his wife and children to devote himself to her. She enjoyed torturing him during sex sessions, burning his body with cigarettes. Yet another of her victims was

Count Pavel Kamarovsky who insisted that she marry him. She agreed, but only after he insured his life for her benefit. He was dead within a month; shot by

RIGHT: Countess Tarnowska, who was found guilty of conspiring to kill her lover Count Kamarovski after persuading him to take out a life insurance policy which would pay her if he died.

BELOW: Count Kamarowski, who was to become the victim of his wife's heartless scheming.

Naumoff. Marie had led her masochistic lover to believe that Kamarovksy had insulted his virility and honor in various letters.

The fact that Kamarovksy had died so soon after insuring his life inevitably raised suspicion, and the Italian police arrested Marie, Naumoff, and Prilukoff (who had helped draft the fatal letters) in 1907. Their trial began on May 14, 1910, by which time the scandal of the killer countess had sparked outrage at every level of society. A lynch mob waited for her arrival at the

courthouse, and the gondola that brought Marie and her two lovers to the court was greeted by mobs shaking their fists and screaming. When she tried to step onto shore a group of women dragged Marie to the edge of the canal, shouting, "Drown her! Drown her!"

ABOVE: Nicholas Naumoff, who was so infatuated with Marie Tarnowska that he deserted his wife and children to be with her.

RIGHT: Countess Tarnowska arriving at court in Venice under a police escort for her own safety.

Guards from inside the courthouse were forced to rescue the accused!

At the hearing, Prilukoff and Naumoff blamed their actions on their infatuation with the countess, while Marie Tarnowska threw herself on the mercy of the court. She wept copiously and promised to devote the rest of her life to a convent and good works if the jury would just be lenient. The performance saved her life. Pronouncing the verdict, a spokesman for the jury said, "We reject the theory that she was mad. But we find that her mental faculties were partially destroyed." Marie was sentenced to eight years in prison; Prilukoff to 10 years in solitary confinement; Naumoff to three years in prison because he was "suffering from a partial mental collapse." One newspaper reported of Marie, "She is not yet thirty but at least six men have ruined themselves for her; two of these met tragic deaths and four of them deserted wives and children."

For a time, the prison chaplain and jail keepers in Venice treated their prisoner kindly, smuggling in

cigarettes and good food for the aristocratic prisoner. But after the chaplain found an "extremely improper" novel in her cell she was transferred to a much harsher prison in Rome to serve the remainder of her sentence. Still she used her sexual power over men, and her besotted lawyers were able to have her sentence reduced: Marie was released after five years.

She later committed suicide, but before she took her own life made an announcement that became legendary, saying "I am the most unfortunate woman in the world. I am a martyr to my own beauty. For any man to behold me is for him to love me. The whole pathway of my life is strewn with the bodies of those who have loved me most."

Michael Telling

Although there can be never be a good excuse for killing another human being, it is difficult not to feel a pang of sympathy for Michael Telling. Already of a fragile state of mind before he married for the second time, his vicious wife did everything in her power to send him over the edge. And when he inevitably snapped, she reaped the harvest of her bitter tongue.

All of Michael Telling's family wealth couldn't buy him a happy childhood. While he may have had everything he wanted in terms of material things, his violent alcoholic father and a cold, unloving mother left him emotionally scarred by the time he reached maturity. A failed marriage did nothing to help, but after he met Monika Zumsteg while on holiday in America and again fell in love his inner turmoil would reach boiling point.

He could not have picked a worse match than his second wife. Almost as soon as the wedding was over, Monika turned on her husband. Her days and nights were spent languishing around the couple's British country home in West Wycombe, Buckinghamshire, drunk and high on drugs, and for entertainment she taunted her husband. She told him that he was sexually inadequate, that she had only married him for his money, and that she had taken lovers both male and female: anything she could think of that might wound the man she had married.

For a brief period the couple seemed to realize just how destructive their problems were. Monika joined Alcoholics Anonymous, and Telling admitted himself to a psychiatric hospital, but it was to no avail. Back at home the pattern of their relationship quickly reasserted itself, and Telling was finally pushed to breaking point by the woman he both adored and detested. On March 29, 1983, as Monika sneered at him yet again, he grabbed a rifle and shot her. Telling left the body where it lay for two days before dragging it into a bedroom and then spent the next few days talking to his wife's corpse. Finally, some semblance of sanity returned and he was forced to deal with the situation. Friends were told that Monika had run off, and Telling made a long distance drive to the South West of England to dump the body after first having removed Monika's head in an attempt to stop the body being identified. Unfortunately for him, the expensive clothes that she was still wearing gave the police the vital clue they needed when the body was discovered and when they searched Telling's home Monika's decomposing head was found in the garage. "I just snapped" was all he could say.

At his trial the prosecution attempted to portray the killing as a cold-blooded, premeditated murder. They presented Telling's careful covering of his tracks as evidence that he was brutal, but sane. The case of his defense counsel, however, was stronger. Backed up by psychiatrists' reports and the testimonies of his friends and family, they showed that Telling was seriously disturbed. Even his mother took the stand to tell of her son's troubled childhood and suicide attempts and as the court heard of the verbal abuse that he had suffered from his wife, Telling gained some small measure of sympathy. When the time came to give their verdict, the jury acquitted Telling of murder but found him guilty of manslaughter on the grounds of diminished responsibility. He was sentenced to life imprisonment.

Harry Kendall Thaw

An obsessive, violent man of unrestrained appetites, Harry Kendall Thaw may have married the woman that he had relentlessly pursued, but he never forgave or forgot his former rival for her affections; the man who stole from her what he had wanted for himself—her virginity.

Thaw was the son of a wealthy Pittsburgh coal and railroad baron. While his mother later claimed that her son had been trouble from the day he was born, Thaw's father secured him places at private schools, the University of Pittsburgh, and, later, Harvard University. Nevertheless, Thaw squandered the advantages that came with the best education that money could buy. He preferred a wild life of gambling and chasing women and was eventually dismissed from university after chasing a taxi driver with a loaded gun.

Moving to New York City, Thaw began taking drugs and hanging out with chorus girls in Broadway shows. He also became friendly with the famous architect Stanford White with whom he shared a passion for showgirls. The friendship was short-lived though; it soured when Thaw discovered White had made sarcastic remarks about him and his ability to impress women. Thaw's hatred for the architect deepened when White showed an interest in Evelyn Nesbitt, a chorus girl from the show Florodora who had also caught Thaw's eye.

Although White warned the showgirl about his former friend, Thaw continued to pursue Evelyn, presenting himself as a considerate suitor. During an illness, Evelyn was hospitalized, and Thaw visited her regularly, also taking the opportunity to ingratiate himself with her mother. Meanwhile, White's interest in her waned, leaving the way clear for Thaw to woo Evelyn (and her mother) with promises of a luxury lifestyle. Eventually, the strategy paid off and Evelyn agreed to marry him. But it was a tainted victory for

Thaw. When Evelyn accepted the proposal she also confessed that her virginity had been lost to Thaw's rival, Stanford White.

Thaw's reaction was extreme. He took Evelyn to an isolated castle in Germany, raped her, and beat her mercilessly. Astonishingly, the marriage still went ahead—possibly because by now Evelyn was too scared of her fiancé to break the engagement off. The newlyweds settled in Pittsburgh with Thaw's mother.

On June, 25, 1906, they made a visit to New York City. That evening they went to Café Martin to dine. Thaw immediately spotted Stanford White and soon learned that his wife's former lover was to attend the premiere of stage show *Mam'zelle Champagne*, a show the Thaws were also planning to see that night.

Following dinner, a seething Thaw took Evelyn back to their hotel and disappeared, returning just in time to pick her up and head to the show. Curiously, he wore a large black overcoat though it was a hot evening. At the rooftop theater of Madison Square Garden, the hat check girl tried to relieve Thaw of his heavy coat but he refused to take it off. The couple were shown to their table where Thaw appeared distracted. He could not sit still but wandered through the crowd during the show, approaching White's table several times only to back away again. Then, during the show's finale song, *I Could Love A Million Girls*, Thaw walked up to Stanford White and fired three shots at close range into his face, killing him instantly.

At first, the crowd first thought the shooting was part of the show, but as realization dawned that Stanford

White was actually dead, Thaw—holding the gun aloft—walked through the crowd and met Evelyn at the elevator. When she asked what he'd done, he replied that he had "probably saved your life."

Thaw stood trial for murder twice. At the first, from January to April 1907, the jury could not reach an agreement. At the second in January 1908, Thaw pleaded insanity. In an effort to protect her son, Thaw's mother set out to corrupt the trial. She offered Evelyn a million dollars plus a quick divorce to testify that White had abused her, and Thaw had simply been trying to protect his wife from an evil man. Evelyn did just as she was asked, perjuring herself in court with the skill of a professional actress.

Thaw was found not guilty by reason of insanity and thus escaped the death penalty, though he was incarcerated at the Mattawan State Hospital for the Criminally Insane in Fishkill, New York. Here, he enjoyed almost total freedom and in 1913 Thaw took the opportunity to escape, walking out of the asylum to a waiting car that drove him over the border to Canada. He was quickly extradited back to the United States and two years later a jury judged him sane. Thaw was released after serving just seven years in a comfortable institution. Nevertheless, he soon tangled with the law again. In 1916, he was accused of sexually assaulting and horsewhipping a teenage boy. Again declared insane, Thaw was sent to another asylum where he spent seven years before regaining his freedom once more in 1924.

Thaw died of a heart attack at the age of 76 in Miami, Florida, in February 1947. He left $10,000— less than one per cent of his wealth—to his former wife for whom he had once killed. Having trusted the Thaw family, Evelyn never did receive the million dollars she had been promised for her part in helping her violent husband evade justice.

Charles-Louis Theobald, Duc de Choiseul-Praslin

The scenario of a man growing weary of a wife and taking a younger lover is a familiar one. But while such stories usually involve heartbreak and emotional anguish, few end as tragically as that of the Duc de Choiseul-Praslin, Charles-Louis Theobald.

ABOVE: The Luxembourg Palace in Paris, where Charles-Louis Theobald committed suicide while awaiting trial for the murder of his wife.

The aristocratic **Duc de Choiseul-Praslin,** had married his wife Fanny when she was a dazzling young beauty of just 19. But as the years passed and Fanny gave birth to their 10 children one after another, she put on weight and her famous looks deserted her. Perhaps if her husband had loved her as he should, she would have entered a cheerful old age delighting in her family and not caring about her fading beauty, but the duke could not be content with his aging wife. He tormented her with a series of barely secret affairs. The latest in a line of young women to tumble into his bed was the family governess, and this time the duke was more in love than ever. Yearning to be free of the miserable Fanny, his thoughts turned not to divorce, but to murder.

On August 17, 1847, the Choiseul-Praslin family spent the night at their house in Paris. At 5am, servants heard screams from Fanny's room and rushed to her aid, believing burglars had broken in. They knocked at the locked door in vain. Now all was quiet. The servants ran to the garden in a bid to catch the intruder. When they returned, empty handed, Fanny's bedroom door had been opened. Inside was the duchess, dripping with blood and propped up on the bed. Her throat had been cut and her face beaten to a pulp with a blunt object.

Suspicion immediately settled on the duke, who had been nowhere to be seen during the commotion.

Police searched the house and soon unearthed the blood-stained handle of a dagger, a blood-stained bathrobe that someone had tried to wash, and a leather sheath. Also discovered were pitiful letters from the duchess to her husband begging him to end his affair with Henrietta and listing his previous lovers. A loaded pistol was found by the duke's bedside. The evidence suggested that Choiseul-Praslin had first intended to shoot his wife but realizing this would be heard, attempted a silent death by cutting her throat instead. However, the incompetent killer failed to sever her windpipe with his first slash allowing Fanny to raise the alarm by screaming.

The duke's guilt was further proclaimed by blood stains found in his bedroom wash basin and bite marks on his leg that his wife had given him during her struggles. Staff also told police of the violent arguments between the couple and how, during one, she had threatened to leave her husband.

Pathetically, the duke protested that he had tried to defend his wife from the intruders, but his flimsy story fooled no one. After being held under house arrest, he was transferred to the Luxembourg Palace in Paris pending trial by the Court of Peers. However, on August 18, 1847, while in custody, he took advantage of a guard's absence to poison himself with arsenic. Even on his deathbed, the Duc de Choiseul-Praslin denied all accusations.

Norman Thorne

A plain woman, Elsie Emily Cameron was not used to receiving attention from men, so when Norman Thorne made advances toward her she quickly gave him her heart and her body. And when he decided that he didn't want to marry her after all, she was so distressed that she felt the only way to keep him was to lie.

Elsie Cameron and Norman Thorne met in 1920 while she was working as a typist in London and he was an electrical engineer. At only 18, he was nine years her junior, but he didn't seem to be put off by the difference in their ages and nor did he seem concerned about Elsie's spectacles or the fact that she wasn't a great beauty. Flattered by his attentions, Elsie fell in love. Thorne had ambitions beyond being an engineer and

RIGHT: Chicken farmer Norman Thorne standing amongst his birds at Crowborough, Sussex, on the exact spot where the remains of his missing fiancée Elsie Cameron were later found buried.

wanted to run his own business. Accordingly, he bought a small piece of land at Blackness, Crowborough, Sussex, and set up Wesley Poultry Farm, working hard to make it a success between rushed visits to Elsie. When he converted a farm shed into living accommodation, Elsie began traveling down to Sussex to see him and during the Christmas of 1922, Thorne proposed and was accepted.

Elsie's happiness wasn't to last though. Soon after they became engaged, Thorne's business began to fail and pleading financial difficulties he refused to set a wedding date. The situation was further complicated when he met a woman called Bessie and decided that he preferred his new lover to his fiancée. In October 1923, Elsie traveled down to Crowborough and, as usual, stayed with neighbors. She spent a week with Thorne but her intuition told her that his feelings had changed. When she returned home to London, she wrote a letter telling her fiancé that she was pregnant in a bid to hurry the wedding. Thorne's reply was not what she expected. Cornered, he confessed that he tired of her and told her about Bessie.

Distraught, Elsie rushed to Thorne's farm and arrived unannounced on the morning of November 30, 1923. To calm her, Thorne relented and said that he would marry her and she returned to London hoping that the future she had so longed for was still just around the corner. The following week, Thorne's father visited the farm that week to discuss his son's finances and offer some advice. He warned Thorne to be cautious over Elsie's claims of being pregnant and told him to write to her and discover the truth. When she received the letter, Elsie became even more desperate than before and on Friday December 5, 1923, she again caught the train to Crowborough station from where she walked to Thorne's farm.

Five days later Elsie's father sent a telegram to Thorne asking after his daughter. Thorne replied that he had not seen her. The next day Mr Cameron informed the police of his daughter's disappearance. They found that Elsie had been seen by two flower-growers while walking toward the farm at about 5.15 pm on the last day that anyone had seen her. Thorne, however, remained adamant that Elsie had not been to the farm. By the beginning of January there was still no sign of her, and police began questioning Thorne's neighbors, one of whom said she had seen Elsie entering the farm on the day she had vanished. Sussex police requested assistance from Scotland Yard and officers decided there was enough evidence to arrest Thorne and search the farm. Elsie's watch, bracelet, and jewelry were found in a tin and the attaché case she had been carrying was later found buried near outbuildings.

Thorne denied murdering his unwanted fiancée, telling police interrogators that he and Elsie had argued over his relationship with Bessie. He had stormed off and later returned to find that Elsie had hanged herself from a beam with his washing line. Fearing that no one would believe his story, Thorne said he cut her down, chopped off her legs and head, and buried the parts under his chicken run. However, a postmortem showed no signs of rope marks and Thorne was charged with murder.

The case came before Lewes Assizes on March 4, 1925. Thorne's defence argued that the postmortem report was flawed, telling the jury that creases on Elsie's neck may have been made by a rope. The police countered this by testifying that there was no sign of a rope having been suspended from any of the farmhouse beams. Twelve days later the jury returned a guilty verdict. Thorne was hanged on April 22, 1925, the day that would have been Elsie's 27th birthday.

Jean-Pierre Vaquier

When British inn owner Mabel Jones took a vacation in Biarritz, France, in 1924, she wasn't the first married woman be carried away by the holiday atmosphere and the suave charm of French men. But what was for her a simple vacation romance turned into a dangerously obsessive love for the man she left behind.

Leaving her husband Alfred to run the Blue Anchor Inn in Byfleet, Surrey, Mabel Jones headed for the south of France and a well-deserved break. She booked into the Hotel Victoria and soon fell in with a dapper, bearded Frenchman called Jean-Pierre Vaquier who was working there. He was a skilled technician and delighted guests at the hotel by arranging the transmission of music concerts into the hotel's salon. The debonair Frenchman was also soon delighting Mabel in different ways. The couple had a brief, but very passionate liaison.

All too soon it was time for Mabel to return home, and she bid her lover a fond farewell, thinking that would be the last of the matter. She was mistaken though. Back in England, Mabel received a telegram from Vaquier asking when it would be convenient for him to call on her. She ignored it and was startled when after she had been home a month Vaquier arrived at the

inn. While she had finished the affair with no regrets and just a few happy memories, Vaquier's love had blossomed into a driving obsession and now he wished to claim her for his own. Mabel was forced to have furtive meetings during which she tried to make it plain to the Frenchman that his attentions were unwanted, all the while looking over her shoulder to make sure her husband didn't notice Vaquier ardently attempting to woo her. Feeling guilty for the lengths he had gone to out of love for her, she didn't charge him for his stay, and it was explained to Alfred Jones that Vaquier was waiting for money to arrive to pay for his "business trip."

Vaquier's love was not to be so easily turned aside and he took it into his head that if Alfred was to be taken out of the picture, Mabel would return to his embraces once more. On March 1, 1924, Vaquier went to London and bought strychnine, signing the poison register "J. Wanker." Now familiar with Alfred Jones drinking habits and noticing the fact that he habitually took indigestion salts as a hangover cure in the morning, Vaquier spiked Alfred's bottle of medicine. On the morning of March 29th, he watched as Jones swigged from the bottle and then helped carry him to his bedroom when he became ill. Alfred Jones died in agony some hours later.

The sudden death prompted a postmortem during which Alfred's body was found to contain strychnine. Both Vaquier and Mabel were questioned and a photograph of the Frenchman was published in various newspapers. The chemist who had supplied Vaquier with the poison recognized his face, and the Frenchman was arrested at a hotel in Woking, Surrey, then charged with murder. Although he maintained his innocence throughout the trial at Guildford Assizes in July 1924, Jean-Pierre Vaquier was found guilty and hanged at Wandsworth Prison, London, on August 12, 1924.

ABOVE: Jean Pierre Vaquier, who in 1924 poisoned Alfred Jones, proprietor of the Blue Anchor Inn in Byfleet, Surrey.

Picture Credits

Getty Images
4, 7 David McNew
8, 9, 10 Topical Press Agency
11, 12, 13 Keystone/Hulton Archive
15, 16, 17 Edward Gooch
20 FPG/Hulton Archive
24 Yvonne Hemsey
25, 26 Topical Press Agency/Hulton Archive
27 E. Dean/Topical Press Agency/Hulton Archive
28 General Photographic Agency/Hulton Archive
30, 31 Leon Neal/AFP
33, 34, 41, 43 Popperfoto
44 Express Newspapers
49 William Frederick Yeames
50 Sotheby's London/AFP
51, 53 Topical Press Agency
54 STF/AFP
55 Mike Nelson/AFP
56 POO/AFP
57 Lori Shelper/AFP
58, 59 POO/AFP
60 Myungh J. Chun/AFP
61 Hector Mata/AFP
67, 69 William F. Campbell/Time Life Pictures
71 Fotos International
73 Archive Photos
75 Popperfoto
76, 82 Fox Photos
83 Topical Press Agency
84, 85, 88, 89, 91 Kirby/Topical Press Agency
92 E. Bacon/Topical Press Agency
94 Topical Press Agency/Hulton Archive
95 Firmin/Topical Press Agency/Hulton Archive

Press Association
21, 45, 46, 47, 63, 64, 65 (both), 68, 78, 79, 81.